D0442513

WHEN GOD FIRST THOUGHT OF YOU

Other books by Lloyd John Ogilvie

Drumbeat of Love
Life Without Limits
Let God Love You
Lord of the Ups and Downs
If I Should Wake Before I Die
A Life Full of Surprises
You've Got Charisma
Cup of Wonder

WHEN GOD FIRST THOUGHT OF YOU

THE FULL MEASURE OF LOVE AS FOUND IN 1, 2, 3 JOHN

Lloyd John Ogilvie

WORD BOOKS

PUBLISHER
WACO, TEXAS

All Scripture quotations, unless otherwise noted, are from the Revised
Standard Version of the Bible, copyrighted 1946, 1952, © 1971, 1973 by the
Division of Christian Education of the National Council of the Churches of
Christ in the U.S.A., and used by permission. Quotations marked TLB are
from *The Living Bible, Paraphrased* (Wheaton: Tyndale House Publishers,
1971) and are used by permission. Quotations from *The New English Bible,*
© The Delegates of the Oxford University Press and The Syndics of The
Cambridge University Press, 1961, 1970, are used by permission. Quota-
tions from *The New Testament in Modern English* (revised edition), © J. B.
Phillips 1958, 1960, 1972, are reprinted with permission of Macmillan Pub-
lishing Co., Inc.

Printed in the United States of America
ISBN 0–8499–0102–2
Library of Congress catalog card number: 78–64793

To John Davies

*who took an insecure
high school student and
helped him believe that
nothing is impossible*

Contents

Preface

Writing this book has been like carrying on a deep conversation with a trusted friend. I've pictured you in my mind's eye. The many faces. Fellow adventurers in my congregation in Hollywood. Others with whom I have shared profound fellowship in retreats and conferences across the country. Church leaders who have confided their hopes and discouragements. People with problems, anxieties, and needs. Authentic people daring to live the abundant life without reservation. All God's people. A gift to me.

I listened to your voices as I took time to be quiet, reflect, and write. Voices with questions which resist easy answers, with longings which defy glibness, with yearnings for forgiveness and a healing of memories, and with aspirations for visions and dreams which cannot be quenched. You have trusted me with your inner heart. And, I have heard your voice from the deep. This book is my response.

I keep a daily log in which I jot down what people ask, share, or confide. It's a journal of the journey of faith we are privileged to share together—a constant companion when I seek to sort out the fresh implications of the Scripture for life today.

Two years ago my own devotional reading in the Scripture led me back to the Apostle John and his letters to the churches in Asia Minor. What he wrote to his cherished friends has the ring of comtemporary reality. I should not have been surprised, but I discovered that the Beloved Disciple and Apostle of Love had dealt with most all of the questions, difficulties and frustrations I have heard you express and that we've empathized over together. The idea of a book was born. I wanted to listen to John with one ear, you with the other, and God with my mind and heart. What I have written is the result.

The stages of preparation flowed naturally. Months of poring over the Greek text deepened my understanding of what John had written and heightened my excitement over the impact of his message for us today. A series of sermons preached to my Hollywood congregation refined and polished what my exposition had excavated. The writing of these chapters with you in mind was the sheer joy of the conversation you have initiated.

The Christians to whom John wrote were beset by beguiling distortions of the Gospel. Gnosticism, with its subtle denials of the incarnation and equivocation about the triumphant adequacy of Jesus Christ, were stretching and tearing the fabric of the fellowship. The struggling Christians needed to be sure of Christ and his love for them. Most of all, they needed to love themselves and each other as much as the Lord did. Near the end of his life, John dipped into the wells of his experience with Christ as disciple, apostle, and senior saint and poured out his heart in personal intimate conversation about what it means to abide in Christ and have Christ abide in us. Each verse inspired by the Holy Spirit is an arrow of truth and hope for us today. John's purpose was to share the magnificent vision of what we were like in the mind of God when he first thought of us. My hope is nothing less for all of us.

The chapters of this book are arranged so that we can have a daily conversation with each other, with the Apostle John, and then with God. I hope the thirty chapters will enable one of the most exciting and liberating months of your life. Each chapter is salted with questions and discussion starters which will make the topics viable for small groups as a guide for study and interaction.

The typing preparation of the manuscript was a team effort. Gwen Waggoner, my administrative assistant, was tireless in her encouragement of my writing, as well as typing and retyping revisions. Stephanie Edwards MacLeod, an outstanding television communicator in her own right, typed several of the chapters as an expression of friendship. Betty Parrish also assisted in the typing. I owe a debt of gratitude to these friends.

My wife, Mary Jane, has been a vital part of my conversation with you, the reader, in these chapters. She shares my delight over the special opportunity to offer this book as a tangible expression of our love for Jesus Christ and you.

LLOYD JOHN OGILVIE

1.

When God First Thought of You

That which was from the beginning, which we have heard, which we have seen with our eyes, which we have looked upon and touched with our hands, concerning the word of life.

1 John 1:1

READ: 1 John 1:1–4

It had been a difficult week. One of those "Who am I, what am I doing here, is it all worth it?" kinds of weeks.

We all have them. Everything piles up. Nothing goes the way we'd planned. People frustrate us. Our goals seem strangely distant and elusive. Work loses its sparkle and zest. A dull blandness engulfs us.

At the end of a week like that, a friend said a liberating thing to me: "Lloyd, I want your life to be as beautiful as it was in the mind of God when he first thought of you."

I was deeply moved. The words penetrated my mind and then the depths of my heart. The affirming admonition tumbled about inside me as if trying to gain control of my consciousness. A few hours later, when I was alone and quiet, I gave the reorienting vision of my friend's words full attention.

Prayer. More than a monologue. A dialogue in the depths.

"Lord, what was I like when you first thought of me? What did you intend my life, all human existence, to be?"

13

Quiet. No answer. Yet the silence was itself an answer. Like a conversation with a true friend who allows you the freedom to talk until you know what you want to say.

I tried to imagine life as God had intended it—before we messed it up, twisted it with selfishness and pride. It was a sublime moment of getting back to basics, awakening again to reality.

Reality? Yes! The week I had been through was not reality. It was a blue funk of distorted reality.

My mood began to change.

More quiet. I was not alone. The Lord was answering my prayer. The answer was himself!

A thought was his first gift to me. It leaped to the center of my consciousness and took command. Excitement surged through me. Warmth. Light. Conviction!

The room in which I sat praying was dim with the fading light of late afternoon, yet there was a brightness that contradicted the time of day. The dimness of my soul was being flooded with light, with the illumination of a rediscovered truth which became an experience.

"Christ! Christ, Lloyd, Christ! That's how I first thought of you. And that's exactly why I came in him. Not only so you would know what I am like. But that you could know my picture of what you were meant to be!"

My consciousness dilated. The focus was Christ himself. Purpose and power in a Person. I was drawn back into companionship with the Lord. The secret of being all that I was meant to be when he first thought of me was fellowship with him. The more he became the centering force of my thought and feelings, the more I would become like him in action and reaction.

I was a different person when I finished praying. My problem had not been my schedule, the pressures of living, or the people of my life. I was the problem! I had drifted off center. For a few days I had entertained the arrogant, unproductive thought that if circumstances or people would change according to my will and strategy, life would be beautiful. That was not the frustration. It was I!

This was not the first time I had been through such a week, nor will it be the last. The difference now, as a result of my friend's vision and my time of prayer, is that I know what to do. Christ himself is the difference. And I don't have to wait days, or even hours, to get back to him. The practice of the picture. Recovering what I was like when the Lord first thought of me right now! Forgiveness. Acceptance. Unchanging love. A new beginning.

That's what John wanted to happen in his beloved friends. The warmth of the first-person assurance is captured by the Living Bible paraphrase of 1 John 1:1: "Christ was alive when the world began, yet I myself have seen him with my own eyes and listened to him speak. I have touched him with my own hands. He is God's message of Life." The aged and seasoned apostle had learned it himself through years of experience.

Life began for him when he first met Christ and the Lord called John to follow him. The brief years of ministry with him had been adventuresome and exciting. From the first time he saw him, he could not take his eyes off him. All through those days of triumph and tragedy, John had felt a special love and tenderness from the Master—the closeness of trusted friends; yet something more, much more.

The "disciple whom Jesus loved" became John's second name. Was it because he was more sensitive and receptive to allow his heart to beat with the cadence of the Lord? Or was his special gift the realization of how much he needed his Master?

Don't forget that Jesus called him "a son of thunder." No gentle, artistic dreamer, this John. His heart was as tumultuous as the seas on which he had sailed and fished. He was impatient and ambitious. He vied for power and struggled for his own identity with the other disciples. But he was open about it. Perhaps that's why Jesus loved him. John seemed to be the first to discover that the life Jesus called them to live could not be lived without trusting, dependent companionship with him.

That's why John took the crucifixion so hard. An excruciating hopelessness had replaced the joy of closeness with the Lord. He could not make it without the Master.

No wonder the resurrection was everything to John. When Mary Magdalene stuttered out the inexplicable fact of the empty tomb, John was astounded. What did it mean? He had to see for himself. His legs could not carry him fast enough as he ran from the Upper Room to Joseph's garden. Listen to his own words: "We ran to the tomb to see. I outran Peter and got there first, and stooped and looked and saw the linen cloth lying there. . . . Then I went in too, and saw, and believed that he had risen—for until then we hadn't realized that the Scriptures said he would come to life again!" (John 20:3–5, 8–9, TLB).

Repeated appearances of the resurrected Lord sealed the triumphant experience for John and began a new level of relationship with Christ. At Pentecost, when the Lord returned in the presence and power of the Holy Spirit, John received a closeness and oneness with Christ that exceeded anything he had known before or immediately after the resurrection. Christ became his abiding, indwelling, empowering companion. Christ was life for John!

But that life had not been easy or placid through the years. Hardship, persecution, and difficulties punctuated his days. But through it all, the living Lord had never left him alone. From exciting days of the expansion of the church, to his imprisonment on Patmos as a political prisoner, to the prolonged years of ministry among the churches of Ephesus and the Lycus Valley, John's vision of the Alpha and Omega, "the A to Z, the Beginning and the End of all things" (Rev. 1:8, TLB) had been the center and source of life for him.

The first sentence of John's letter to the early church communicates who Christ is and what he has done. He is the creating and communicating God. In his Gospel, John called him the Word, the Logos, the wisdom and power of God who was the first creative cause of everything. "Before anything else existed, there was Christ, with God. He has always been alive and is himself God. He created everything there is—" (John 1:1–3, TLB). Christ was God incarnate revealing what we were like in the mind of God when he first thought of you and me. That's why who he was and is, said and says, is the ultimate point of reference for the shaping of our lives. John put it simply: "He is God's message of Life."

Closeness with Christ is the inspiration and intimation of our living. A personal relationship with Christ helps us to see both our distortion of his intention and what we are to become. It was not easy to be a Christian in ancient Ephesus, nor is it now in your city and mine. The same distracting philosophies which disturbed the Christians then, trouble us now. We are tempted to make Christ an idea or theory which has little to do with our difficult weeks or days or hours. We share with the Christians to whom John wrote the seeming disadvantage of not having seen Christ in the flesh. But we can know him with the same intimacy John knew after Pentecost.

If you had a choice of being ushered back through history to be part of the band of disciples to walk and talk with Jesus in the flesh, would you want that more than knowing his presence and power in intimate friendship for your life today? I choose the latter. More than an example of life, we have the Enabler of Life who can reproduce himself in us.

That's what I need for today! What about you?

PRAYER FOR THE DAY: *Living Lord Christ, God with us, you created us and have come to us to make us like yourself today. We want our lives today to be as beautiful as they were in your mind when you first thought of us. Amen.*

2.

The Recovering of Intimacy

If we walk in the light, as he is in the light, we have fellow-ship with one another.

1 John 1:7

Illus:

READ: 1 John 1:5–10

One afternoon I watched a Japanese freighter being unloaded in the Los Angeles harbor. I love the sea and ships. As I sat there observing the gigantic crane lifting crates of merchandise out of the hull of the ship and lowering them down on the wharf, I did not expect a word from the Lord. I should not have been surprised. He often talks to me when I least expect it and through very unusual situations.

I noticed that each container had handling instructions stamped on the side in bold black letters, in both Japanese and English. I suspected that something had been lost in the translation. What was printed may have been ambiguous to the stevedores working with the cartons, but it was a clear message from the Lord to me: "If this side is up, this container is upside down!"

I laughed. Then I began to think about what the words meant for my life and the people I love. "If this side is up, this

18

life is upside down!" How could I tell if my life was right side up? What are the identifiable signs that we are accomplishing the purpose for which we were born? Or what would be the undeniable marks of missing the reason we're alive?

I returned to my study of John's letters to the Asian churches with fresh vigor. In 1 John 1:5–10 he gives us an incisive inventory to discover the purpose of our existence.

We were created for an intimate relationship with God and one another. Few words are as misused and misunderstood as *intimacy*. It implies so much more than just romance or sex. An intimate relationship is one which is distinguished by close association, contact, familiarity. Personal. Innermost. Intimacy implies an intrinsic encounter, one which reveals and relates the essential nature and inner being of two persons. The intricate I meets the real you.

John wrote his letter to help his friends recapture intimacy with God. In the opening of his letter, he declared that in Christ, God had opened and revealed his intrinsic, essential, innermost heart. God had dwelt bodily in Jesus. The eternal life of God was revealed in time and space for all time and for all people. Nothing had been left out or held back. He had made the first move toward his people. Out of unreserved love he had offered himself. "In him was life and the life was the light of man" (John 1:4). The Light of the World revealed both God and man. In that illumination, men saw God as he is and themselves in their need of him. The purpose of it all was fellowship with God and a new quality of fellowship between those in whom the light had shown.

Many of the people who read John's letter had experienced the glory of the Light and had begun to walk in him. But the vision had grown dim with the passing of time and the virulent infection of the Gnostic heresy. Unsettling questions had raised doubts: How could the pure Spirit of God dwell in human flesh? Was Jesus only one of many manifestations of the light of God's truth? If God is unblemished goodness, how can he enter into the sordidness of human need? The result was uncertainty and a dulling of spiritual sensitivity among the Christians. For the intimacy they had once known with God and each other was being substituted a bland intellectualism.

Long before John wrote those words, the Lord had given him a personal word for the Ephesian church which exposed the problem. I think that was on John's heart as he wrote this urgent recall to intimacy. While imprisoned on Patmos, the Lord had appeared to him with profound concern for the churches. The complaint against the Ephesian church could be applied to all churches and to most Christians in any age: "I have this against you, that you have abandoned the love you had at first" (Rev. 2:4). The intimacy of their first love for the Lord and each other had been disturbed and weakened. An aloof coolness had replaced the closeness and warmth they had known when they had first fallen in love with Christ and had discovered the delight of Christian fellowship in the church. The spontaneity and adventure had been lost. Stiffness, suspicion, pretense, judgmentalism and dishonesty resulted. That's the reason why, in this section of his letter, John called his friends to a rediscovery of the joy of an honest, open life. In so doing, he gives us the most magnificent description of Christian intimacy ever written.

Intimacy is rooted in honesty. It is the exposure of our inner selves to the searching light of God's truth. God knows us completely. So why try to hide what we are or have done? But we do. We think he will love us only if we are good. When we are less than good, which is most of the time, we pretend that we are something we are not. The dishonesty of duality results: we put up a front of righteousness, while inside we are a tangled web of distorted ambitions and frustrations, memories of the past, and fears of the future. The Lord wants to get beneath the surface to the real person who lives in our skin. The tragedy is that we can profess Jesus Christ as Savior without allowing him to be Lord of our innermost thoughts, fantasies, plans, and purposes. We are no different than the people to whom John wrote. The most subtle manifestation of Gnosticism is to come to believe that God cannot invade our sinful humanity and transform our inner minds and hearts. John speaks to our condition. Guilty as charged! "If we say we have fellowship with him (our Lord) while we walk in darkness, we lie and do not live according to the truth" (v. 6). Walking in darkness is simply excluding the Lord's light of truth and judgment from illuminating any aspect of our inner or outer lives.

I spend my life with people. Many of them come to me to find the dynamic power of Christ in their lives. Most of the people who are deadlocked in problems have not discovered that our Lord is able to take any problem we will entrust to him and transform it into a potential. So much of our life is untouched by the power of his Spirit because we try to live on our own insight and strength. We say we have fellowship with him, but all of the crucial commitments and concerns of our lives have never been surrendered to him. Often we admire the freedom and joy of other Christians and want what they have discovered. It's no secret: they have allowed the light of Christ's presence to give perspective and power to their perplexities.

Honesty with God means constantly inviting him to take charge of all our relationships and responsibilities. Any area of life which we have not consciously committed to him and opened to his light will be an area of darkness. We walk in darkness when the most crucial things in life are unexamined in the light of Christ's Lordship. If our career, sex life, money, family, self-image, hopes and dreams have never been opened to him, our Christianity and churchmanship are an eloquent lie. That's the reason for the lack of power in so many Christians today and in dull, bland churches.

I talked over lunch recently to a man who had lost the power he had experienced when he first met Christ. He explained that all the excitement was gone. As we ate, we tried to discover what had happened. He was doing all the outward things which can keep a relationship with the Lord vital and adventuresome. Daily prayer, church attendance, witnessing to friends were all done with ritual obedience. But the fire was gone. In an effort to get to the raw nerve of what was wrong, I asked some penetrating questions.

"Is there any place in your life where you are saying 'No!' to God's guidance? Are there areas of your life in which you have resisted his invasion and inspiration? Are you hiding anything from God or any other person? What thoughts, inner feelings, and memories have been unexposed to the light of God's searching truth?"

The man's response was alarming. "You've got me on all counts!" His life was a pitiful picture of the dishonesty of duality. He was one person on the outside and another on the inside. All his energies were being expended on keeping up the pretense of being a committed, evangelical Christian. His relationships at home were a disaster and his inner thought life was a mess he knew God could not bless.

After he had allowed me to know the real person inside and I had confided some of my own struggles to be an authentic person, he exclaimed, "Wow, do I feel better. At last someone knows the real me! God has known all along, but somehow telling someone else has helped me want to really tell him how much I want to be different."

We prayed together in unstudied, nonreligious language. Then we made a covenant to meet regularly together. He was determined to take the painful but liberating steps toward being an honest Christian. That meant allowing the Holy Spirit to penetrate the innermost dimensions of his nature. It also meant allowing people to know him. He soon found that people had been pretending with him because his assumed "togetherness" set up barriers against vital communication.

What happened to this man is what John longed for in the lives of his friends. He was urgently concerned about the Christians who said they had fellowship with God but were walking in darkness. That problem has been around for a long time. It's the most disturbing cause of spiritual ineffectiveness and ineptness in the church today. There's no lack of people who say they believe in Christ. Why, then, is impotence the condition of so many Christians? We have missed the intimacy with the Lord he intended. That means allowing his light to infiltrate our memories, hidden thoughts, and secret desires. The darkness of our souls needs the exposing light of the Spirit's judgment, healing, and redirection. Walking in the light begins in our intricate hearts.

I'm left with questions you may wish to share. Have I allowed God to know me absolutely and utterly? Like you, I have ambitions for my life I need to reveal to the Lord. So often I make my plans, dream my visions, and ask the Lord to empower them. Repeatedly I have had to relearn that God provides only for what he guides. Also, there are feelings and attitudes about people and life I nurse in the darkness of my mind. Does the Lord know? Of course he does! Why, then, do I allow them to fester? Eventually they must be exposed and confessed. Why do I wait musing in the darkness of the emotional prison of my own making? Why do you?

There comes a time when we can't say we love God and exclude him from the real person inside any longer.

John brings us to that point. If we say we have fellowship with God and set up a picket line around our hearts, we lie and do not live the truth we talk about so piously. Until we allow God to get at the core of us, to the vital nerve center of our guarded thoughts and feelings, there will be no intimacy.

Now John moves on to compare walking in darkness with walking in the light. What a difference! "If we walk in the light, as he is in the light, we have fellowship with one another, and the blood of Jesus his son cleanses us from all sin." The result of intimacy with God is a profound intimacy with others.

The greatest impediment to deep communication is religious pretense. Authentic relationships are built on the foundation of shared needs, not adequacy. We do the same thing with people that we have done with God: we think we will be accepted and loved only if we measure up. The result is that we pretend. We say the right things and try to do the accepted and required action.

Remember the relief you felt when some admired hero of your life revealed some failure or need in his life? Human after all! Or, can you recapture the warm feelings of being able to help someone who has shared with you a problem you've been through? Fellowship in Christ is the result of mutual need for forgiveness and grace.

Walking in the light enables us to be vulnerable with others about what we've discovered and are experiencing of the acceptance of our Lord. When we have to put up an image of perfection, we negate the Cross and make fellowship an impossibility.

I have discovered that the people who are closest to the Savior are most aware of their need of his unmerited favor. A sign of maturity in Christ is the expressed desire and need to grow. The most advanced saints I know are able to identify with the failures and frustrations of others.

The recipients of John's letter were constantly being challenged by the elitist philosophies. No wonder he wrote the shocking words, "If we say we have no sin, we deceive ourselves, and the truth is not in us." John's words must have given comfort and assurance to the struggling Christians under attack from those who claimed an esoteric, exclusive knowledge of God, unavailable to others. The authentic, sure mark of a vital Christian is that he is aware of his next steps of growth and is able to share his viability with others.

One of the greatest obstacles to intimacy in the local congregation in America is our unwillingness to talk about our own problems and needs. The result is that the gospel is proclaimed, but our aching hearts are not healed. We come to church longing to find help, but little is said about the hurts and hopes we all feel. Preaching is conceptual; teaching is unrelated to life. The Lord seeks to invade our inner jungle, but that will not happen until someone is real enough to tell us what Christ has done in his own life. Great preaching must include an exposure of what's happening in the preacher. True fellowship is enabled by a mutual sharing of what Christ has done and is doing in the complexities of life.

As I read John's concluding words in this section, I feel the pulse beat of God's imploring love: "If we confess our sins, he is faithful and just, and will forgive our sins and cleanse us from all unrighteousness. If we say we have not sinned, we make him a liar, and his word is not in us."

Sin is to miss the mark. That's the basic meaning of the word. More than little wrongs, sin is separation from God. It's running our own lives, trying to live on our own strength, and planning our lives within the limits of our own meager resources. Sin is whatever keeps us from intimacy with God and other people. Willfulness and pride. Privatism. Selfishness. All our sins are rooted in the basic sin of trying to be a diminutive god for ourselves and others.

John offers two alternatives as to what to do about our condition. If we say we have no sin, we negate the reason Christ came and resist the forgiveness he died on the cross to offer us. But if we admit whatever it is in us that keeps us from the intimacy we were created to experience, forgiveness is given even before we ask. Quite an offer! All we have to do is confess our longing to be right with God and to be free of the habitual patterns which exclude him from our lives. Then we can list out all the sins we have committed in the exclusive darkness of self-determined, arrogant independence. What a tragedy it would be to live our lives and miss the experience of the liberating love that forgiveness enables.

I don't know about you, but that alarms me into a new desire to allow the light of God's presence into my whole life and relationships. Our longing for intimacy can be satisfied. It begins with God and will pervade all of life. Unless that's up, our lives are upside down!

PRAYER FOR THE DAY: *Holy Father, thank you for creating me for an intimate relationship with you and others. I confess my sins which keep me from you and others. If you know me as I am, help me to be what you intended. Forgive my pretentious dishonesty with people that leads them to think I am more than I am and shuts them up in a prison of self-condemnation. Help me to be open and honest about what I am discovering so that authentic fellowship can be experienced. Amen.*

3.

Bottom Line Is Always Red

Anyone who says he is a Christian should live as Christ lived.

1 John 2:6, TLB

READ: 1 John 2:1–6

Bottom line is always red for a Christian. Outgo must exceed income. When it comes to giving ourselves away to others in creative, healing, forgiving love, our relational books will never be balanced. Love is a careless spendthrift when it comes to the needs of people—regardless of what they do in return! We are called to give more of ourselves to others than we either expect or demand to receive from them. If we take Jesus seriously, we will be in the red.

Look at the unpolished directness of John. He exposes our carefully balanced ledgers of giving as much as we get, of loving those who love us, of parceling out affection in cautious proportion to what we have received from others. Our black, balanced line of neat quid pro quos suddenly embarrasses us.

"Anyone who says he is a Christian should live as Christ lived." There's the motive and method of living in the red. Verse 6 of chapter 2 is the distilled result of John's years of

27

fellowship and experience with Christ. It was the message of his life.

We quickly check other translations of the Greek. The impact is the same. There's no escape; none of them let us off easily. The Revised Standard Version says, "By this we are sure we are in him; he who abides in him ought to walk in the same way he walked." We pause to think about the way he walked. The road led to Calvary. The Phillips translation offers no easy evasion: "The life of a man who professes to be living in God must bear the stamp of Christ." The same cutting edge is in the New English Bible: "Here is the test by which we can make sure we are in him; whoever claims to be dwelling in him, binds himself to live as Christ himself lived."

Our audit of Christ's balance sheet is alarming. Bottom line is red! He came as God's gift; he gave himself away; he recklessly invested his whole life for you and me. The cross is the plus mark against the debits of our deliberate sins. All we have to offer him is our failures and rebellion. He did not love in proportion to the love offered him. No bartering lover, this Jesus! He was misunderstood, misused, and mistaken. Neglected by some; negated by others. Betrayed by those who followed him; beleaguered by those who feared him. Love was his only response.

John had Calvary on his mind as he inventoried the incarnation. Two key words—one from verse 1, the second from verse 2— are seared into John's psyche. Christ is our advocate with the Father, the expiation of our sins. "Advocate," the term used in traditional translations, translates the Greek word *paraklēton*. It has three main uses.

It means to comfort. Jesus said that he would send the comforter, the Holy Spirit. By that he meant that after his death, he would return and that his ministry would be to comfort. But not at an uninvolved distance.

The second use of the word is for one who stands beside us, who is called to our side in time of need for strengthening. The two aspects blend together: Jesus comes to us and he comforts us. But the comfort is never conditioned by our character.

The third aspect of John's use of *paraklēton* exposes the active nature of the comfort. It means one who pleads a case. The Lord's comfort is not a "now, now, don't fret!" but a penetrating reconciliation. Jesus Christ the righteous, assures our forgiveness and absolution. When he intercedes for our absolution, we are restored, released, regenerated in him.

This means he relates to us now as he related to people in need during his ministry and comes to us with forgiving assurance.

But that's not all! More than that, he is the expiator, the propitiation for our sins. The word is *hilasmos,* a sacrificial word. It means the placation or pacification of one who is offended or insulted. Also, the word means forgiveness. But most of all, it implies the complete removal of guilt. C. H. Dodd's metaphor is that it disinfects. The third of these meanings clarifies all the others: Jesus forgives us not just as a placation of the justice of God, but as an act which establishes us as accepted as if we had never sinned. Righteousness is the gift of a right relationship as if it had never been broken.

That's how much Christ loves you and me. The books are always unbalanced. He has done so much more than we deserve or could ever earn. We are constantly in his debt. Bottom line is red because of you and me! Written in red blood is "Paid in Full."

This is the way Christ walked, lived, and lives! Nothing we have done or do conditions his comforting presence. He comes to us, stands with us, pleads for us, absolves us, and cleanses us.

Now John gives us the acid test of whether we have accepted this and are in the flow of continuous experience of it. "And how can we be sure that we belong to him? By looking within ourselves: are we really trying to do what he wants us to do? Someone may say, 'I'm a Christian; I am on my way to heaven, I belong to Christ.' But if he doesn't do what Christ tells him to, he is a liar. But those who do what Christ tells them to will learn to love God more and more. That's the way to know whether you are a Christian" (vv. 3–5 TLB).

As Christ was always in the red, so must we be. The implication of doing what Christ tells us to do is obedience. "As the Father sent me, I send you." That means doing what he did and joining him in what he is doing. The key words *advocate* and *expiation* focus the length and depth that we are to go for people. We are to make the first move, stand beside people, take their cases on our hearts and plead for them with prayers of intercession. When we express forgiveness, we are to relate to people as if they had never committed the act, spoken the cutting word, or failed in some responsibility. Of course, we do not repeat the advocate's expiation but reproduce it by communicating its efficacious dynamics, not only in word, but attitude.

The challenge is:

1. Get next to people.
2. Strengthen them with Christ's strength.
3. Pray for them.
4. Mediate his forgiveness.
5. Make it real through our own acceptance.
6. Relate to them as forgiven people.

That's what John means when he says we should walk, live, communicate as Christ did. It gives me marching orders for today and all my tomorrows. What about you?

We hold our unbalanced books out before him. People have not returned our love; some have returned evil for good. Now he looks not at the unbalanced bottom line but into our eyes and on into our hearts.

"Would you do less than I did? If I had done to others what they did to me, you would not have a cross and an empty tomb. What would you do now or for eternity without that? Even so, love one another as I have loved you!"

PRAYER FOR THE DAY: *Lord, help us to get into red on bottom line. Forgive our carefully settled black on the ledger of our lives. Help us to become involved in the needs of people today regardless of what they do or say. Most of all, we praise you that you always make a deposit of strength and courage to help us more than meet the overdraft of discipleship. Through Christ, who helps us to live as he lived. Amen.*

4.

What Have You Done Lately?

I am writing you a new commandment which is true in him and in you, because darkness is passing away and true light is already shining.

1 John 2:8

READ: 1 John 2:7–11

I zoomed into a service station about out of gas. The Andy Devine-sized attendant sauntered up to my car. I rolled down the window and said, "Fill 'er up!"

The man looked at me as if he should know me. After he connected the gas pump, he cleaned my windshield. I noticed that he kept looking at me in an effort to identify where he had seen me. Trying to be friendly, I smiled. He smiled back with a quizzical look. After he finished filling my tank, he came to my car door window to collect.

"I know you! Don't tell me; let me guess. You're in the movies, aren't you? Or is it television?" And then with the familiarity of hero buffs, he talked to me like an old buddy about the fact that he was sure he had just serviced the car of a famous entertainment personality. Finally he said, "Ah, come on; tell me your name. I'm sure I've seen you in the flicks or on the telly."

I told him my name and introduced my wife. "Lloyd Ogilvie!" he exclaimed, as if he had just met Jimmy Stewart. He didn't recognize my name, but was still convinced that I was some star.

"Great to meet you!" he said. "What have you done lately?" He expected a scoop about a new contract.

I was tempted to tell him I was between pictures. Honesty won out. "I'm between sermons!" I responded, with a lilt of humor in my voice. But no amount of explanation would dissuade my new friend. Even an invitation to attend my church did not break the spell of the star-struck movie-lover. To this day, he's probably chuckling about the incognito star who tried to pass himself off as a clergyman!

As I drove off, my tank was filled with gas, but my mind was filled with that question: "What have you done lately?" That started a good inventory. It motivated me to think about my life and what I was accomplishing in all that I do.

The Apostle John gave the early Christians a basis for such an evaluation. The purpose of his letter was to remind them of Christ's basic commandment. "Beloved, I am not writing you a new commandment, but an old commandment which you had from the beginning; the old commandment is the word which you have heard. Yet I am writing you a new commandment, which is true in him and in you."

John is thinking of Jesus' commandment in John 13:34–35: "A new commandment I give to you, that you love one another; even as I have loved you, that you also love one another. By this all men will know that you are my disciples, if you love one another."

The commandment was old and yet very new. It can be found in Leviticus 19:18: "Thou shalt love thy neighbor as thyself" (KJV). Jesus made it the basis of the new life in the kingdom of God. He initiated it as a new commandment in that he actually called people to live it. His whole life incarnated it.

The Christians to whom John wrote had heard the commandment from the first day they had learned about Jesus Christ and the gospel. So it was not new in that sense. The word the Apostle used for new was one that refers to quality rather than chronology or quantity. The commandment was qualitatively new in that the Old Testament law, reaffirmed by Jesus' message and life, is constantly new for the believer. We never outgrow the commandment. It becomes new each time we allow its challenging plumb line to fall on our relationships. The Christian life is a million new beginnings instigated by the fresh challenge to love others as Christ has loved us. It is the reorienting verity in the midst of conflict. It is our mandate when dealing with difficult and impossible people. However much we are hurt or disappointed with people, the commandment becomes Christ's new command about what we are to do.

Doing love is the difference. The Leviticus commandment had been around for hundreds of years. It was repeated with ritual regularity, ossifying the living vitality into the dry bones of words without action. Jesus *did* the commandment. He redefined the meaning of neighbor as all of God's people, and clarified love as knowing no limits. He loved Hebrew and Samaritan alike. His love reached out to the sinner. Finally, he was crucified not for the words he spoke, but for the indefatigable love he expressed.

John called the Christians back to the basic commandment not as a lovely platitude but as a basis of action and daily living. It's in the doing of costly love that the commandment is new again.

Driving home from the service station that night, evaluating what I had done lately, I was very aware of people who needed my love. Not all of them are easy to love. Some make it almost impossible. The Lord's words rumbled in my soul: "Love as I have loved you." How often I had learned that! And yet, the words were fresh orders from the Master for the next day.

Truth is not a proposition to be grasped by the mind only; it is something to be lived. Alfred North Whitehead said, "Truth is the correspondence of appearance with reality." It's when what appears to be is seen in the light of reality. Christ is reality for us, the ultimate test of what we believe and do. That's what John means when he says, "The darkness is passing away and the true light is shining." The old commandment becomes new each time we see the truth of Christ pierce the darkness of prejudice and preconception. In the light, we see people for what they are in their need. As the darkness lifts, the reality of a person is exposed, and we are challenged anew to *do* love.

For John, light equals love, and darkness equals hate. The dawn has come in Jesus Christ, and the darkness is already passing away. That's true through the historical advent, incarnation, and resurrection victory, but it's also true for each of us every day, as Christ dawns on each perplexing situation and problematical person. The night of our perception passes as the Morning Star rises in the horizon of our minds. When the Son of God dispels the night with the dawn of truth, we can see what the loving thing is that must be done, and do it by his power in us.

The words in the epistle are sharp and alarming: "He who says he is in the light and hates his brother is in the darkness still." The claim to be in the light is contradicted whenever we hate a person. Hate is symbolized by darkness. Anyone who hates lives in the darkness.

All of this would be generalized admonition if it were not for the special word John uses as the subject for either love or hate. He's referring to more than people in general. He uses the word *adelphon*—"brethren," fellow believers in Christ. That stabs us awake to the deeper meaning of the passage, John was actually dealing with a problem of Christians hating one another in the church. How could this be? Before we smack our lips in consternation, we need to look at the relationships of some Christians today, and then at our own hatreds.

Hate is a strong word. The Greek word used for *hate* in this passage means enmity, hostility, animosity, and prejudice. The checkered history of Christianity keeps us from being too critical of those Christians to whom the epistle was addressed. All we have to do is flip through the pages of the development of the Christian church in America to see that the old problem is still around. The conflicts between Roman Catholic and Protestant, and the squabbles between the denominations of Protestantism are not pleasant to review. Then we look at the factions in any local congregation. John's letter could have been written for us!

But let's be personal. This book is between you and me. We started with a commitment to be honest with each other as we sorted out the implications of John's epistles. Whom among the brothers and sisters in Christ do we hate? My first reaction to that is to recoil defensively. Then, when pious protestation subsides, I realize that hate, for me, is an absence of active love. There are people who have hurt and spitefully misused me. Any leader is a moving target for criticism and judgments. I keep reminding myself that you can't please all the people all the time. But when a person zeroes in on you as the bull's-eye for his vitriolic anger, the desire is to return the fire with a double bolt. People do a lot of what they do because of what's going on inside them. Often we have not been the original cause of the disturbance, but have ignited the fuse of the powder keg in their emotions. When they say and do the hateful thing, my temptation is to cut them off and leave them to fume, incarcerated in their own prison. But what they need is love, and not a return of hate.

As I write this, I am trying to be as incisive with myself as I hope you will be when you read it. Is there anyone I hate? The word bites. I don't want to use it. But many of the synonyms for *hate* help me get hold of the implication of John's challenge for me. I find that there are people I hold at arm's length or avoid contact with because of my feelings about what they have said about or done to me. I can hide in the righteous indignation, affirming that I did not initiate hostility or aversion. My problem is how I react to it. Enmity is cancerous. It begets its own kind. The thing the Lord has put on my heart is the necessity of becoming a person who can return love for hate rather than hate for hate.

How do you feel about what I just wrote? Can you identify? Are there people in your life who have pulled you down to their level of darkness? Light and darkness are equally contagious. Can you think of anyone whom you would rather not see again? How about those feelings which surge within you when you think of or are encountered by certain people? Who are the *adelphon*, the brothers and sisters in Christ, with whom differences, conflict, and competition have caused a broken relationship? I can empathize. It's not pleasant to have someone rummage around in our sublimated, repressed feelings. Some of you may wish you had skipped this chapter. We would rather nurse our wounds alone, justified by our perception of the people who have been able to contradict our picture of ourselves as loving, forgiving, gracious people.

In each relationship where love has been distorted, I find the Lord is giving me something to do. A letter, a phone call, an act of involved love—each perfectly suited for the person— becomes clear. My ability to abide in the light is at stake. It would be so easy to evade the challenge, to straighten out the Lord about the fact that I am a victim of the other person's confused thinking or immaturity. He's not impressed.

As I read on in the passage, I realize how crucial our conversation in this chapter is to you and me. "He who loves his brother abides in the light, and in it there is no cause for stumbling." The word *stumble* is *skandalon* in Greek. It's a biblical metaphor for a protruding stone which causes a traveler to trip. Jesus used the word in two ways. He spoke of himself as a *skandalon* for those who are self-righteous. He also used the term for anything that would trip a person in following him.

In this passage from 1 John, the two uses blend together.

Hatred for fellow Christians is a stumbling block. Those people become a cause for our tripping in our strides to grow as Christ's disciples. But the Lord told us that he would meet us in the lost, the lonely, and the imprisoned. The people who disturb and distress us are placed in our path by Christ himself for us to love in the power of his love. If we refuse, we trip on the Lord himself.

The darkness of animosity makes the path treacherous, but Christ's light makes stumbling stones into stepping stones. When we ask the Lord for the specific strategy for doing love in each troublesome relationship, he illuminates the person so we can see not an enemy but a person desperately in need of healing and hope. He shows us the inner cause of the problem beneath the word or action which caused us to feel hostility. The particular thing he tells us to do will touch the deeper level.

I find it's good to set a time line on our reconciling action. When will we be able to do the loving act? Set it carefully. At the end of tomorrow or next week the Lord will be waiting with that same disturbing question. "What have you done—not just lately—but when you told me you would do it?"

PRAYER FOR THE DAY: *Loving Lord Jesus, your commandment to love as we have been loved is unsettling. It would be so much easier to memorize your new commandment and repeat it with lovely tones. But you want action. Your light has illuminated people we find it difficult to love, and whom we even hate at times. The word* hate *sticks like a bone in our throats. We find it painful to tell you about our attitudes. And yet, the pain of being out of fellowship with you is far more excruciating. Lord, teach us how to* do *love. Amen.*

5.

Always Beginning, Constantly Adventuring, Forever Secure

I am writing to you ... little children, ... fathers, ... young men.

1 John 2:12–13

READ: 1 John 2:12–14

The stages of life—we all go through them. Someone has said that there are four stages of life: childhood, youth, young adult, and "you look wonderful." We know we have hit middle age or beyond when people say "You look wonderful" instead of "Hello." The ambiguous comment may cover a multitude of wrinkles and gray hair.

Illus: *aging*

Being able to enjoy the stage of life we're in is not easy. So much of life is lived in anticipation of the next stage. Psychiatry tells us that if we skip a period of natural growth and experience, we spend the rest of our lives trying to recapture it. The popularity of all the "passages" books indicates that we all long to understand why we react the way we do at each stage of our development as people. There are some of us who are old in attitude and reaction long before our time, and others who never grow up. To be mature in one's growing years

39

and viably youthful as we grow old is the challenge of adventuresome living.

John wrote to three groups of Christians in the churches in Asia. He addressed the little children, the young men, and the fathers. The usual tack of interpretation of this passage is that John wrote to three different groups. I want to shift the sails a bit, to catch the winds of the Spirit about this passage.

Every congregation has newborn babes in Christ, those who are the energetic growing Christians, and others who are the mature, seasoned saints of God. The tragedy is that we lose the best of all three stages. We often lose the excitement and dynamic warmth of the first experience of being loved just as we are. Remember when you first experienced the joy of falling in love with Jesus Christ? How easily the delight of the new birth is lost in routine churchmanship and traditional Christianity!

But the experience of growing up in Christ is no less satisfying. The reckless abandon of daring to follow Christ at all costs should be everyday Christianity until the day we die. There is a quality of discipleship which takes the Master seriously. We want to follow him and communicate his love to others. And then, a truly mature Christian who knows the Lord in depth, and knows from experience that he is faithful in all life's circumstances, is a work of God—beautiful to behold and know.

The challenge is to keep together the excitement of becoming a Christian, the daring of growing up in Christ, and the ripened depth of mature personality under the control of Christ. We need the best of all three stages of Christian growth. John gives us the ingredients of each as basic to the experience of all. He wanted some to grow up; others to keep the winsomeness of ever-recurring, fresh grace; and others to take the next steps of being Christ's person.

My interpretation of this passage follows Augustine and others closely. John was trying to capture the basic ingredients of each stage of Christian growth and urged the Christians to never lose the best of all three.

The quality of the children in the faith which we should never lose is forgiveness. "I am writing to you, little children, because your sins are forgiven for his sake." The experience of forgiveness is the nutritious milk for new babes in Christ. We are set free of the sin and failure of our old life. Acceptance by God through Christ and the Cross helps us grasp the amazing fact that the old is gone and we have made a new beginning. I can still remember the freshness and freedom I felt when I accepted Christ as my Savior and surrendered my life to him. Life began for me that night as a college freshman. It was a triumphant transition in which I became a new man in Christ through the power of forgiveness and liberating grace. I couldn't get enough of prayer, the Scriptures, and Christian fellowship. Filled with boundless enthusiasm for Christ, I wanted the whole world to know the joy of being a new person in Christ.

It wasn't long before the experience of Christ as Savior flamed into the challenge of following him as my Lord. Babies are lovely, but it would be a monstrous tragedy if a person remained a baby all his life. The same is true in the Christian life. Growth in the implications of the Lordship of Christ was demanding and sometimes painful. The thrill of being one of the Master's men also meant the cost of following him. He was up to a great thing in me. My mind had to be repatterned around his mind; my emotions needed healing and release; and my will had to be taught the ways of obedience.

I soon had to come to grips with the power of evil in me and others, and in my world. John understood the challenge of the adolescent and young-adult stages of growing in Christ regardless of the age at which we are "born again." "I am writing to you, young men, because you have overcome the evil one." The implication is not that the battle is completely over, but that there are specific evidences of victory which should give hope and vigor to future skirmishes. The verb form used here, indicating a complete victory after conflict, must refer to Christ's victory over Satan on the cross. We appropriate the resources of that victory each time we confront evil in ourselves, people, and the world. Each new battle is engaged with the knowledge that, if we trust Christ and what he has accomplished, we too will have victory.

Spiritual adolescence, regardless of our chronological age, is a necessary and unavoidable part of growing in Christ. We are never finished with it, really. But there is an indomitable decisiveness in adolescent Christians who are determined to be disciples. Nothing seems impossible. How quickly we lose that. The vigilant desire to be completely Christ's person enables us to go through the rewarding, remedial period of Christian growth. Our personalities must be reformed. Habit patterns must go. Ways of reacting to people which debilitate them must be crucified in us. Memories which haunt and hurt our living at maximum have to be healed. The "old man" in us must be purged and purified.

Satan is not concerned with us until we become new people in Christ. A growing Christian is a vulnerable target for his negative, humiliating attacks. The evil one does not let go of us easily. He is the motivator of self-doubt, equivocation of our commitment, and resistance of our calling to be to others what Christ has been to us. The battle is on. The only way to win is to grow deeper in our relationship with Christ. The hand of Jesus is more powerful than Satan's insidious virulence. We belong to Christ. He will not let us go. That's the source of our victory in each new conflict, as we seek to be all that our Lord created us and called us to be.

The danger is that we are tempted to think that the growing years of our Christian life can be finished. Our Lord is at work helping us to be pioneers all through the years of our lives. We are called to be adventuresome, vigorous, daring, "the best-is-still-to-be" followers of Christ right up to the end.

Abraham Lincoln said that every person over forty is responsible for his own face. That's true of the physically mature. It's also true for our spiritual lives. We are responsible for what we have done with the opportunity of being with Christ. In the spiritual realm, our face is our personality. John addresses the fathers: "I am writing to you fathers, because you know him who is from the beginning"—an apt description of the eternal, creative Word of God. Christ was with God, came from God, and is the source of the beginning of the new creation. The One who is from the beginning keeps us vital and flexible by constantly giving us fresh beginnings.

The Apostle seems to expect that there should be a discernible result of knowing Christ through the years. That forces us to question the ways in which we are different because of companionship with the Savior through life's agony and joy. Paul challenged people to grow up to "mature manhood, to the measure of the stature of the fullness of Christ; so that we may no longer be children, tossed to and fro and carried about with every wind of doctrine, by the cunning of men, by their craftiness in deceitful wiles. Rather, speaking the truth in love, we are to grow up in every way into him who is the head, into Christ" (Eph. 4:13–15). Maturity in Christ is becoming like Christ in thought, action, and reaction.

Age does not insure maturity. We all know Christians in middle and later years who are childish, not childlike in Christ. Some have never grown beyond the first infant steps in Christian growth. They are still fussing with elementary issues of Christianity. A pastor in the Southern Baptist Convention complained that he had the largest cradle roll in his denomination—most of his members.

There is nothing more disappointing than spiritual senility. Instead of adult-sized issues and challenges, a person can regress to infantile, simplistic obscurantism. We can major in the minors, cripple the movement of the local congregation, and long for the "good old days." The problem is not just among the chronologically old. I talked to a twenty-seven-year-old crotchety Christian the other day. He had been a

Christian for twelve years. He refused to grow up emotionally and spiritually. Lack of spiritual maturity is usually expressed by the absence of both the enthusiasm of the new Christian and the daring of the growing disciple.

I am very thankful for some members and leaders in my congregation who are mature in years and Christian character. A long life in Christ has produced an admirable combination of irrepressible hope, ready-for-anything openness, discernment salted with love, and inclusive receptivity to new people and innovative ideas. They are examples to all of us of what Christ can do with a person who is completely yielded to him.

Sanford Marmaduke is a constant source of affirmation and encouragement. His love for Christ, deepened by years of study and prayer, shines radiantly from his face. He's a father and brother to the people of God. As a lay elder in the church, in charge of candidates for the professional clergy, he has guided several hundred men and women into creative ministry. I asked a long-time member when Sandy became the mature Christian he is. The response would have pleased the Apostle John. "Why, Sandy has been that way for as long as I've known him, and that's over fifty years. I guess you don't have to be old to be mature in Christ!"

William Barclay has a vital summary of John's stages of Christian growth. "All Christians are like little children, for all can regain their innocence by the forgiveness of Christ. All Christians are like fathers; like full-grown, responsible men, who can think and learn their way deeper and deeper into the knowledge of Jesus Christ. All Christians are young men, with glorious and vigorous strength to fight and win their battles against the tempter and his power. It seems . . . that indeed is John's wider meaning."[1]

---

[1] William Barclay, *The Daily Study Bible, The Letters of John and Jude* (Philadelphia: Westminster Press, 1960), p. 62.

The Christian life is always beginning, constantly adventuring, forever secure. It is for each of us to decide where we are in the Christian life. Some of us may still be babes and need to grow up. Others are in the thick of the battle to be faithful and obedient as Christ's disciples. Still others are enjoying the security of having grown to maturity in Christ. I want to keep the best of all three stages for all years. If we can never lose the initial joy, keep a daring discipleship, and become more mature in every day we are privileged to live, we will have the abundant life Christ lived, died, and is with us now to make maximum.

The new life in Christ will be exciting all the way up if we put him first in our lives. How to do that is what John deals with next.

PRAYER FOR THE DAY: *Creative Lord of growth and new life, we praise you for all three stages of life. Help us to keep all three as we live our days. We long to stay fresh and vital with daily experiences of forgiveness. Give us the power of your Spirit to confront and overcome the frustrations of life. And enable us to grow up to full maturity in every aspect of our faith. Thank you for calling us to an adventure in which we are always beginning, constantly growing, and profoundly secure. In Christ our life and Lord. Amen.*

6.

How to Survive in a World Like This

Do not love the world or the things in the world. If any one loves the world, love for the Father is not in him.

1 John 2:15

READ: 1 John 2:15–17

One of the most difficult challenges for a Christian is to live in the world without the world living in him. How can we live in vital union with Christ and still live in the pressures of the world? It's not easy. The world has its value system, its idea of success, and its beguiling temptations. Geraldine Farrar, former prima donna of the Metropolitan Opera, stated it clearly. "So much is pressing in on humans today that they do not have time to stand still long enough to evaluate live. They gulp life and taste nothing. They eat life and have no savor."

The purpose of this chapter is to "stand still long enough" to evaluate our relationship to the world. Jesus said that we were to be in the world but not of it. Our task is to understand what that means. Or, in the words of Arlo Guthrie in *Alice's Restaurant*: "I've got to discover my thing and do it quickly!"

Dietrich Bonhoeffer counseled that we should discover a

holy worldliness: we should live in the world but as God's called, chosen, and Spirit-filled persons. Our survival in the distorted dehumanization of the world is dependent on it. Christianity is not a "cloistered virtue" to be lived in monastic, safe aloofness. "By Christian this-worldliness," said Bonhoeffer, "I mean living unreservedly in life's duties, problems, successes and failures, experiences and perplexities. In so doing we throw ourselves completely into the arms of God."

Our problem is the temptation of throwing ourselves into the arms of the world and not God. We can be captured by the world as we live in its perplexities and problems; we can be sucked into its measurement of a happy life. We all live in two worlds—the inner world and the outer world. The question is, how can we allow the inner world of our relationship with Christ to guide our activity in the outer world? Just the opposite happens to many Christians. The values and purposes of the outer world dominate our ability to grow in Christ.

We promised each other honesty as we deal with the thorny issues that trouble us. How well do you do in being faithful to Christ in the world? In what areas has the world invaded your thinking, plans, and purposes? I must be frank with you about my life. I live in a fine home, serve a large church, work in a community that worships success at all costs, feel the same quest for achievement as anyone, and want to enjoy the days of my life as much as everyone else. Now, how can I earn a living, save, and spend as a faithful disciple of Christ? When does prosperity negate Christ's power? In what ways do my desires to make it in the world end up with the world having made me?

The late Mayor Daley of Chicago was quoted as saying, "We are moving from higher platitudes to higher platitudes." I do not want to do that with you. We do not need more pious platitudes, but a clear word about how to love God more than we love the world.

The problem is not unique to our century. The Apostle John tackled it to help the early Christians live in the real world. It was no easier then than now.

At the beginning of this chapter, we read John's admonitions about holy worldliness in the Revised Standard Version. J. B. Phillips's translation of the same passage is very helpful: "Never give your hearts to this world or to any of the things in it. A man cannot love the Father and love the world at the same time. For the whole world-system, based as it is on men's desires, their greedy ambitions, and the glamour of it all that they think splendid, is not derived from the Father at all, but from the world itself. The world and all its passionate desires will one day disappear. But the man who is following God's will is part of the permanent and cannot die."

John confronts us with the world—what it is in stark reality, and how to live in it with Christian integrity.

The word John uses for world is *kosmos*. It means more than the planet on which we exist, more than nature and the created order of material existence. In the New Testament the term *world* has a profound moral implication. It implies life apart from God. The world is any person, relationship, structure of society, circumstance, or situation which has been unredeemed by God's judgment and grace. The world is the fallen creation in rebellion against God. It is humanity which has forsaken God and his plan and purpose. In unified form, the world is society independent from God, government without God's plumb line of justice and righteousness, economic systems without the sovereignty of God, corporate industry without concern for persons or the purposes of God. This is the world in which we must live our daily lives without falling in love with it. The world, in the sense John uses it, has a lot to offer. Infatuation is a constant danger. A romance with the world is fed by the possibility of a kind of recognition, popularity, success, and prosperity. In Jesus' words, we can gain the world and lose our souls.

John gives us the secret of how to live in the world without the world living in us.

1. His first piece of advice is, "Do not love the world or the things in the world." Wait a moment, John! How does that fit with Jesus' statement of the purpose of his life? "For God so loved the world that he gave his only Son, that whoever believes in him should not perish but have eternal life. For God sent the Son into the world, not to condemn the world, but that the world might be saved through him" (John 3:16).

There's no contradiction between John's admonition and God's incarnate love. In fact, the way God loved the world is the way to live in the world as Christians. He loved with independence and freedom. At no point did Jesus buy into the value system, the distorted religion, or the competitive materialism of his time. He resisted the efforts of both his disciples and the leaders of Israel to twist his mission and equivocate his message. The Lord loved the world too much for that. He came to call and reconcile the world to God: to call a new creation, and to liberate people to seek first the kingdom of God in the midst of the world. That kingdom is the rule of God in people's hearts, between them in their relationships, and in their responsibilities to society. He said that the kingdom is within us, amongst us, and coming in full power in the world.

Now we can understand what John meant. As kingdom people, we live in history in the world. Our ultimate love and loyalty is to God. Then we are able to love the world creatively without needing either its accolades or affluence. When we love the world as God did in Christ, we are given marching orders to care for people and introduce them to life as it was meant to be in Christ. Our perspective and ambitions change. With people as the focus of our concern, we can do battle with the false values of society and anything which distorts and dehumanizes persons in their primary purpose to know and love God. We are called out of the world to be equipped to go back into the world as free men and women, able to love the world with compassion and without compromising our convictions.

The only way I know that we can evaluate the kind of love we have for the world is to make an inventory of our dominant desires. What is our basic purpose? Can we write it out in thirty words or less? Are we able to support our definition by the way we live? Ask the people closest to us where we live, work, and spend! We all swing between our love for God and the wrong kind of dependent love for the world.

John startles us with the need to love God so much that we will be able to love the world in the right way. "If any one loves the world, love for God is not in him."

We are given three practical tests for our inventory of the ultimate loyalties by which we live.

The first is the "lust of the flesh." Here *flesh* means more than our physical bodies or sexual expression. Flesh is a biblical term for our humanity. The lust of the flesh symbolizes a life dominated by our wants, with little respect for ourselves or other people. It's the childish behavior found in many adults who want what we want when we want it, regardless of what it does to us or the people around us. When the pleasure principle is fired by selfishness and self-satisfaction, we use people as things.

The world around us not only encourages the lust of the flesh, but parades, packages, and purveys it. What's best is what feels good. It becomes ingrained in our value system. We can say that we are Christian, and yet have our lives dominated by the desire for position and power as ends in themselves. The constant question for a Christian is: what do I really want out of life and what is shaping my values?

The second indication that we love the world more than God is what John calls "the lust of the eyes." This is what we see and want, and what we want others to see about us. It's a life commitment to a highly polished surface, regardless of what's inside us—the ostentation of the outward show in our own vanity fair. This lust of the eyes is the inability to see anything or anyone without wanting it for ourselves as a security symbol. More, more, more! The cry of the hungry heart.

The point is that we try to fill with things, people, and activity the emptiness only God can fill. We long for the new and different, yet we end up old and unchanged. Once again the danger signal for the Christian is sounded. We can attest to our belief in Christ and displace him in our hearts with unsatisfying substitutes. There's nothing wrong with money and the things it can buy. The problem arises when all our mental powers, physical energy, and creative time are spent thinking and scheming about, dealing with and clutching at what we've accumulated. Anything that debilitates our primary relationship with our Lord and cripples the growth of our life in his image is an expression of the wrong kind of love for the world.

The third test of whether the world has invaded our souls is what John calls the "pride of life." A study of these words in the Greek text is fascinating and frightening. Pride is *alazoneia*. It's rooted in *alazōn*, which means a booster. In the language of the drug culture today, it's an "upper." Pride is like a narcotic. It is a false mood-changer, to boost our self-image, and a sedative to anesthetize an honest acceptance of our true selves. Pride produces an illusionary hallucination about ourselves. The word for life used in John's phrase is *bios*—the external aspect of our nature; it is not *zōē*—the true life principle within us. The pride of life is defensive self-aggrandizement over surface qualities or abilities, appearance, or demeanor.

The ambience of the world is competitive and comparative. Pride becomes our defense. We must be better, have more, and achieve more in order to stabilize our ego. It is at base a lack of love. Because we do not love the unique, special person God has made us to be, we pretend and protect ourselves against the anguish of insecurity.

I have discovered that praise is the only antidote to pride. The new freedom I'm experiencing is to relish the delight of the gifts and opportunities God has given me. I could not breathe a breath, think a thought, write or speak a sentence,

or be an enabling leader, without God's presence and power.
All that I have and am is a result of his blessing. If he is the
author of it all, I am free to enjoy being me and being used as
a part of the Lord's strategy. Everything he entrusts to us is to
be used for his glory. That realization can heal the pride of
life. Jesus offers us an abundant life filled with love, forgiveness, and joy. When we belong to him, pride is replaced with
gratitude and unrestrained celebration of the capacities,
talents, and gifts he has entrusted to us. We do not need the
booster of pride; that usually leaves us depressed when the
upper wears off and we are alone with reality. We will not be
like the man described by Billy Sunday. He said the proud
person was all front door: when you go in, you're immediately
in the back yard!

Personal check-up time again: Are there any evidences of
pride that indicate that a false love for the world has gotten to
us? Love for God more than the world frees us to live in the
world in the security of the imputed, personal resources he has
given us. Our need for approval will be satisfied by the appro-
bation of God's delight in us. Praise, not pride, is our response.

Finally, John tells us that the world is not worthy of our ultimate love because it's transitory: "And the world passes
away, and the lust of it; but he who does the will of God abides
forever."

The poet Robert Burns knew the fleeting nature of life from
his own experience. A stanza from *Tam o'Shanter* expresses it
vividly:

> But pleasures are like poppies spread:
> You seize the flower, its bloom is shed;
> Or like the snow falls in the river,
> A moment white, then melts forever.

Someone spray-painted the question "What isn't?" on a
dead-end sign. The world is a dead end. When John reminds

us that the world "passes away," he is thinking of the brevity of each person's life on earth, and the instability of anything in the course of history. The only eternal aspect of our life is our soul. How we live in the world now determines how and where we will spend eternity.

PRAYER FOR THE DAY: *Lord God, this passage of Scripture has alarmed us about ways we may have loved the world more than you. Show us the relationships and situations where we have bought into the world's values and priorities. Reveal to us the areas where we are in danger. Thank you for helping us to see that the more we love you, the more we will be free to love the world creatively, without being captured by it. Heal our pride with the power of praise. In Jesus' name. Amen.*

7.

How to Be Present in the Present

Children, it is the last hour.

1 John 2:18

READ: 1 John 2:18

I long to discover how to live fully in each hour as if it were my last hour. So often I miss the enjoyment of the present by rumination over the past, or rehearsal of anticipated problems or joys of the future. Does that ever happen to you? I suspect it does. There may be some comfort for us in the fact that many Christians share our problem of wandering attention.

Recently I took part in a discussion with a group of trusted friends about areas in which we need to grow as Christians. My response was immediate. I confided that I need to learn how to be completely present in the present. That touched a raw nerve in the others. They too found that they miss a great deal of what God has to offer in each moment because they are distracted by what might have been in the past, or by racing ahead to what might happen in the future. We all laughed when the logging-in got around to one of the men who said, "I'm sorry. What were we talking about? I guess I was think-

ing about a crucial meeting I have tonight after this group."
He had not been present at a meeting that was talking about
being fully present! We all can empathize.

There are times when we are in conversation and realize
we've lost the train of thought. Often when we are with
friends or family we find that what we've been through or are
worried about in the next day keeps us from deeply appreciat-
ing them. We fail to listen to or zero in on what people are
saying in words or body language. It's always shocking when a
person tells us that he told us something important and we
can't remember. Some of our most serious goofs are the result
of not grasping the significance of what's told us or happening
around us.

The other day a woman confessed her hurt over the insensi-
tivity of her husband. "I've tried to tell him in a million ways
that I'm lonely, but he's always so distracted. It would be so
wonderful to be married to the other half of my husband that
never comes home with him!"

We can appreciate the woman's criticism. We all have the
same problem with people in our lives. The temptation is to
knock to see if anyone is there. But our criticism is softened
when we realize that often we leave a portion of our minds
elsewhere when we are with people.

We do the same thing with God. It's one of the reasons our
prayers are ineffective. We are not present while we pray. Our
minds wander off to some situation or unresolved tension, and
we suddenly awake to the fact that we've been talking to God
in familiar, hackneyed phrases, while the real person in us is
off fussing with some frustration or being titillated by some
fantasy.

The problem is all the more serious when we think of prayer
as a flow-of-consciousness conversation all through the day's
challenges, relationships, and opportunities. "Prayer without
ceasing" can make the Christian life very exciting. But it
means that we must be wide awake with awareness of what
God is trying to say to us and do through us in each moment.

There are two conceptions of time in the New Testament. One is *kairos*, a point of time; another is *aion*, an age or period of time. We live in duration time for the realization of the *kairos* moment when God breaks through to execute his plan and purpose. The incarnation was a *kairos* event in history. Now in our post-resurrection, post-Pentecost *aion*, God continues to make all of life a *kairos* succession of maximized moments. When he intervenes with blessings or judgment, we face the *krisis*, the crisis necessity to recognize and do his will.

John wanted his friends to know that it was the last hour. I believe he meant more than the end of the world. The terms, "the last days" or the "last hour" are used to signify not only the completion of history, but also the confrontation of God in a crucial time of history.

In the Old Testament, the last days meant a time of special blessing. In Genesis they identify the time when the people of Israel would enter the Promised Land (Gen. 49:1). The prophets looked forward to a time when God would reign supreme and his people would be obedient to him. Even the frightening "Day of the Lord," with its anticipated judgment and destruction, would be the demarcation point of the end of an old age of sin and rebellion, and the birth of a new age of joy and peace.

The church believed that the Messianic age had dawned in the incarnation of Jesus Christ. The early Christians looked forward to the return of Christ imminently, in the second coming. It would be a *kairos-krisis* which would mark the end of an *aion*, and a beginning of a new *aion* in the reign of Christ on earth. The worse things got, the closer they believed they were to the Lord's return.

In that light, we can deal with John's reference, in our text, to the last days. If we assume that he meant the end of history within his lifetime, we must admit that he miscalculated. There are many expositors who use this verse to declare urgently that the end of the world is upon us. That may be true, for the signs of the culmination of history as we know it are startlingly evident today. But our task is not to try to set the hour of the end, but to accomplish God's ends in each hour, to be fully immersed in the present hour as if it were the only hour. When we do that we can be part of the new age God wants to usher into our lives each moment. He is ready to give a new beginning each time we surrender the old syndromes of failure and frustration to him. "Behold, I make all things new!" is promise for any hour we allow to be a *kairos* hour.

Skip down to verses 28 and 29 of this chapter to catch the full impact of what John is saying about the last hour: "And now, little children, abide in him, so that when he appears we may have confidence and not shrink from him in shame at his coming. If you know that he is righteous, you may be sure that every one who does right is born of him." That gives us specifics of how to live to the hilt in every hour. Here's the prescription.

1. Preparation for the second coming is to experience Christ's hourly coming. We will be ready if we are open to receive him now. The interface between now and the end of our life or the culmination of history can be filled with moment-by-moment companionship.

2. Forgiveness of all that is past enables us to be free to live without guilt or remorse in the present hour. We need not be anxious about Christ's invasion of our daily lives if we have nothing to hide. We close him out of our lives only when what we are doing cannot be blessed by him We can be completely open to his advent when the past is healed. Confidence replaces a guilty conscience.

3. Surrender of the future is the key to freedom in the present. Is what we've planned an extension of right-eousness? Can we be right with our Lord and do it? Is it an extension of his will? If so, we can leave the future development of our plans with him. Unworried about what will be, we will be liberated to enjoy all that is available in the present moment.

That's how to be present in the present. What is God saying? What does he want to accomplish? What does he desire to give us? Those are the questions of sensitive saints.

When we ask and allow God to answer these questions in each hour, nothing is bland or ordinary again. All of life becomes a succession of holy hours. Everything from daily chores to praying our prayers becomes an exciting experience.

John identifies the last days because of the difficulties the church was facing. There's a magnificent, liberating truth here. We are tempted to associate times of blessing with success or delights. If that's true, we rule God out of most of our hours. Our life is not all fun and games. We all face hours that are filled with anxiety, difficulty, and pain. We must decide whether these are death throes or birth pangs. John sees them as signs of new hope. When things become the worst, God always gives his best. We can be fully present in life's vicissitudes as well as victories. God is in charge. He will use everything for his glory and to bring us closer to him and each other.

I can't tell you when the end of history will occur, but I can tell you when a new life for each of us can begin. Right now! It's the last hour. Our finest hour. The only hour we have.

PRAYER FOR THE DAY: *Gracious Lord of history, we praise you that our times are in your hand. You know the end from the beginning, blessed Alpha and Omega. Having settled the issue of the end of time, we long to accomplish your ends in time. Thank you for helping us maximize our hours. Help us to be fully present to you and to people, as well as all the delights and difficulties you will use for your glory and our growth. Through Christ our Lord. Amen.*

8.

The Antichrist in the Mirror

So now many antichrists have come. . . .

1 John 2:18

READ: 1 John 2:18–19

A passage of Scripture can be like an island. You have to row around it until you know where to land. It can also be like getting to know a person. A great deal of time must be spent before the person yields his inner self to be known and understood.

1 John 2:18–19 has been like that for me. I thought I knew what it meant and what I wanted to do with it as the basis of this chapter.

My first thought was to do an historical study of the problem of the antichrist in the early church. That would have been a comparatively easy matter of gathering historical and scriptural data about the church's struggle with Satan and satanic influence. But John's reference to many antichrists who had left the church made my study of the passage more relational than conceptual.

The antichrists John refers to were people who had been in

59

the fellowship. More than nameless protagonists, they were people whom John's readers had known and loved in the Body of Christ. Suddenly, I was aware that the antichrist issue was one of deep pain and brokenness for the Christians. Profound empathy replaced my aloof scholarly treatment. The problem of heresy in the primitive church is yours and mine today.

John uses the term antichrist for the first time in this letter in verse 18. He employs it to designate the adversaries of Christ and the church. I have always identified the antichrist with Satan himself, satanic influence, or notoriously evil leaders in history who were archenemies of the gospel. When I personify the antichrist it's usually as infamously diabolical, possessed people. Deeper study of the passage has indicated that the word is also used for divisive and destructive people who are habitually critical, and who diffuse the virulent poison of negative thinking. Let's look at the derivation of the word before we decide.

The word *antichristos* is a combination of the preposition *anti* and the word *christos*. *Anti* can mean either opposition or substitution. Its use in our English words to imply the negative "against" is familiar to us. The idea of substitution provides fresh insight to our understanding of the antichrist. It means not only one who is against Christ, but also one who seeks to put himself in Christ's place. The early church dealt with open, hostile opposition, but also debilitating undermining through infectious infiltration. The latter was most dangerous.

Satan is the original antichrist. He has found ready recruits in every age. His tactics are usually subtle, pervasive, and virulent. John is concerned about Satan's disciples who were disrupting the church. They denied that Jesus was the Christ and that he had lived in the flesh. At best, Jesus was but one of many emanations from God—not the only begotten Son, nor the only way to know God. The denial of the incarnation abrogated the Cross and atonement. Resurrection and hope of eternal life was therefore nullified. If Christ had not lived in the flesh, there was no reason to believe in his living presence and power to aid believers in the problems and perplexities of daily life.

John's concern was not primarily about the blatant, avowed antichrists who were leaders of heretical movements against the church. They could be dealt with in open disputation. What broke the Apostle's heart was the members of the church who had come under satanic influence and denied not only the fact, but the need, of the incarnation. The unexpressed alarm was for others still within the church who were tempted by the false teaching.

That presses us to wonder about the danger of the antichrist today. This passage forces us to be incisive in our contemporary analysis of the beguiling danger. We need to look at verses 22 and 23 as the basis of our judgment: "This is the antichrist, he who denies the Father and the Son. No one who denies the Son has the Father. He who confesses the Son has the Father also." The issue is the incarnation. Anyone who denies that Jesus is the Christ is an antichrist.

The heresy has many subtle forms in our time. There are those who rank Jesus among the great leaders of history, along with Buddha, Confucius, and Mohammed. Others suggest that Jesus taught great insights about God, but was not God incarnate. Still others deny that Jesus' death on the cross was a necessary expiation for our sins. It is possible to teach about Christ, preach his message of love, and follow his exemplary life, without believing in him as our only Savior and Lord.

The greatest concern, however, is for Christians who become antichrists in their substitutions for Christ. C. H. Dodd said, "Membership in the church is no guarantee that a man belongs to Christ and not to the antichrist."

We join the ranks of the antichrist whenever we fill the need for Christ with any of the modern substitutes. Self-justification has many expressions. We rationalize our sins and deny our need for the cross. In reality, we are our own saviors.

God ought to accept us for our goodness, productivity, and faithfulness. Good Friday is a troublesome day; if we had been the only people alive in Jerusalem that day, it would not have been necessary.

Too severe? Check our lifestyles! We live and work as if we can make it on our own. Prayer is spasmodic. Our security is drawn from our positions, popularity, or possessions. Most telling of all is our dumbness about our faith in daily conversations. How would anyone know what we believe? We communicate the impression that what we have and are is the result of talent and hard work.

Others of us swell the ranks of the antichrists by trying to take Christ's place in other people's lives, often with good intentions. We call it love and concern. People grow in dependence on us rather than Christ. Loved ones and friends are implicated in the symbiosis. Our need to be needed prompts us to try to be the answer to people's needs. We insulate people from the reality of their desperate condition. Parents, spouses, counselors, and spiritual leaders all face the possibility of being a substitute for Christ rather than leading people to him.

But the greatest temptation is to be antichrist in our negative thinking and attitudes. The spirit of negativism is infectious. It spreads from person to person. At root, it's lack of trust in the power of Christ. Nothing's impossible for our Lord. Problems are the prelude to his intervention. The Church today needs people who dare to believe that this is still the age of miracles. Christ can change difficult people and transform troublesome problems. We are antichrists when all we see is the human potential in a situation. Criticism is the articulation of negativism. When we resist adventuresome advancement with reserve and caution, we debilitate what Christ is ready and able to do.

Simon Peter was rebuked by Christ when he tried to dissuade him from the cross. "Get behind me, Satan!" was the Master's stern reprimand. It's possible for any of us to be channels of negative influence, masqueraded as sanity and safety.

You and I can be like Peter. We can stand in Christ's way and confuse others about him. The test is what we believe Christ did and is able to do today. We live in a time that desperately needs the radical, to-the-roots communication of the absolute adequacy of Christ and a vivid modeling of what he can do to transform a person's life and meet the problems that face the Church and our society.

The question is: Who's controlling our hearts, Satan or Christ? Jesus' parable of the empty house tells us that reformation is not enough. We need a total regeneration, accompanied by an infilling of his Spirit to fill our empty hearts. Then there'll be no danger of Satan's influence in us or through us. Instead of being an antichrist, we will be part of the Lord's anointed, positive people.

The anointing of the Spirit to occupy our hearts is the subject of the next chapter. The shocking danger revealed in the antichrist presses us on to that with urgency.

PRAYER FOR THE DAY: *Blessed Lord, fill us with yourself. Seal us with your Spirit. Take complete possession of our hearts. Use us as positive agents of your redemptive work in people, the church, and our society. Show us any ways we deny your incarnation or resist your present intervention in people or problems. May we be the first to believe that all things are possible through you. Forgive us any time we are against you, or substitute anything or anyone for you—most of all ourselves. We want to be on your Way and not in the way. Thank you for making us part of the Lord's legions rather than an emissary of satanic influence. We belong to you, Lord. Now use us to your glory! Through the living Christ and the power of the incarnation. Amen.*

9.

Chrisma Comes Before Charisma

But you have been anointed by the Holy One.

1 John 2:20

Read: 1 John 2:20–25

Some months ago Bruce Larson and I took a Rio Airlines flight from Waco, Texas, to Dallas. As we boarded the plane, we noticed the slogan of the airline printed on the side of the aircraft. "Rio Airlines—Your First Step to Everywhere!"

Quite a claim. The small feeder airline had caught its uniqueness in an arresting way. A short flight could be the first step to an international airport, and from there the world was yours.

During the gusty flight on the Texas winds, we talked about what the first step to everywhere was for the two of us. That led me to think about the great need in the church. What was the first step to a revitalization of Christians and a revival in the church?

I still had the first-step-to-everywhere thought in my mind when my studies in 1 John brought me to the amazing assurance in 1 John 2:20: "But you have been anointed by the Holy

One, and you all know." An alternative translation of the promise is, "You know everything."

That's it! The first step to everywhere for a Christian is the anointing of the Holy Spirit.

The Greek word for anointing is *chrisma.* Anointing had a very special meaning in Hebrew history and a grave distortion in the mystery cults. John wrote to his friends to reaffirm the first and by comparison to expose the second.

In ancient Israel during the Exodus, the Lord instructed Moses that the priests were to be anointed with oil. "And you shall take the anointing oil, and pour it on his head and anoint him" (Exod. 29:7). Later, kings were anointed. Samuel anointed both Saul and David. Concerning David, the Lord said to Samuel, "I will show you what you shall do; and you shall anoint for me him whom I name to you." When Samuel saw David, the Lord said, " 'Arise, anoint him; for this is he.' Then Samuel took the horn of oil, and anointed him in the midst of his brothers; and the Spirit of the Lord came mightily upon David from that day forward" (1 Sam. 16:3; 12–13).

The prophets were also anointed in a further period of Israel's history. Their anointing, like the kings, was to set them apart for a task and to give them the special power to do the task. The kings were to rule and the prophets were to bring the message of the Lord's judgment and hope. Isaiah 61:1 is engraved in our memories. "The Spirit of the Lord God is upon me because the Lord has anointed me."

Anointing is the unction of the Spirit of God to impute authority and strength to accomplish a humanly impossible task. The Lord presses us beyond our talent, training, and skill into challenges and opportunities which could not be accomplished without his gifts, wisdom, and enabling power.

The Messiah entered history at the lowest ebb of human impotence. The Anointed One in Hebrew means Messiah. In Greek the word is *Christos.* Jesus was the Anointed One of God and was anointed in a special way at his baptism.

Note the relationship of *Christos* and *chrisma.* Now our

study gets exciting. The Anointed One came so that he could call a people who could be anointed with his Spirit and do what he had done. Our anointing, like that of the kings and prophets of old, is to be set apart for a ministry, and, through Christ, we are given power to live way beyond the level of human capacity.

Key

John wanted his friends to be sure of their anointing so they could combat the false teachings and promises of the mystery cults that were rampant in Ephesus and the Lycus Valley. The leaders of the cults said that their initiation rites gave a person a special contact and closeness with God. They bypassed Christ as the only Son of God and claimed that they could enter the inner portals of God's presence and gain an esoteric knowledge of the divine. It led to exclusion and proud judgmentalism.

John uses a twist on the word *anointing* which roots it solidly in the Messiah. The *Christos* was the only source of a true *chrisma*. The Christians know all that can be given. They need not be insecure or uneasy with the Gnostic heresy or the separatistic cultists. In verse 26 he gives them the confidence they need. "The anointing which you received from him (Christ) abides in you, and you have no need that any one (any of the cult or heresy leaders) should teach you."

Note the immense difference between John's teaching and the teaching of the cults. The mystery religions pressed through the portals seeking to find a special relationship with God with their own mantras and might. The Christians' anointing was the result of Christ's coming to them and abiding in them.

The significant thing for us is that anointing is abiding— our abiding in Christ and Christ abiding in us. The first makes us recipients of the efficacy of his death and resurrection as our salvation. The latter gives us the motivating, engendering, energizing power to live the Christian life. The preposition *in* enables all the difference. I could not live in Los

Angeles as God's man without being in Christ. But I could not do what I am called to do without Christ living in me. John's oft-repeated word *abide* is our guide. We abide in Christ and Christ abides in us. Paul said, "If anyone is in Christ, he is a new creation; the old has passed away, behold, the new has come" (2 Cor. 5:17). The new is Christ himself.

Both the Apostle John and the Apostle Paul were of one mind about the necessity of anointing to live the challenge of life in Roman Asia. Paul wrote about this to the Colossians who lived in the same area and faced the same disruption of the mystery cults: "The mystery hidden for ages and generations but now made manifest to his saints [the church]. To them God chose to make known how great among the Gentiles are the riches of the glory of this mystery, which is Christ in you, the hope of glory" (Col. 1:26–27).

Today we are offered two aspects of anointing. One sets us apart, the other sets us moving. When we accept Christ as our Savior, and this is recognized by our baptism, we are anointed with the Holy Spirit. It is the Spirit who enables us to believe and then comes within us to help us grow in Christ. But that's only the beginning. The second aspect of anointing is the great need among Christians today. When we dare to be faithful and obedient, we are given a special anointing for each demanding opportunity. When we face complexities, we are given wisdom; when we are challenged to love unlovely people, we are given the gift of gracious love; when we are pressed to lead others into the unknown future, we are given vision and guidance. Each stretching possibility brings us back to the Lord for fresh anointing to break ground in the unexplored territory others are unwilling or afraid to pioneer. John said, "Let what you heard from the beginning abide in you." In other words, our initial anointing must be refortified by fresh anointing each day, in each challenge or crisis.

We are having an exciting time in our church in Hollywood seeking to live by the anointing. Some time ago, our elders took a weekend retreat to consider what it would mean to be anointed leaders and be part of an anointed Session Board of Elders to lead the church. Many of the elders had to admit that they thought of their leadership as being the best of human skill and experience they could offer. Some considered the Session a body of capable men and women elected to lead because of previous accomplishment and as a recognition of faithful service and financial support of the church.

We took a prolonged time to study and absorb this passage from 1 John. As the hours went by, we were all deeply moved by the gigantic task ahead of us to be a dynamic church at the center of a great city. We face problems of a changing neighborhood, population shifts, and the insatiable human thirst which can be slaked only by the Water of Life Himself. We have been called to grasp potential, not just solve problems. The Lord is sending us hundreds of new people each year. They need to be introduced to Christ and then helped to grow and be deployed in creative ministry.

It was the exciting opportunity of the future which led us to realize how much we needed an anointing. Individually we acknowledged that we needed the Lord's special blessing. As a group we accepted the fact that we could expect no more of the congregation than we were willing to allow the Lord to give us. This led to some basic commitments. We opened our lives to receive the anointing of the Holy Spirit for our ministry. Then as a unanimous fellowship, we commited the life of our Session to be an anointed band of leaders. That meant being willing to pray for guidance, to plan around the Lord's goals, and to wait patiently for his specific steps of strategy. It's exciting to be part of an implosion which is causing an explosion of new life in the congregation.

Dependence on our skill and talent is an addiction. It's difficult to break the habit. Our first reaction in a crisis is to decide a course of action on the basis of previous experience. Training and experience are valuable tools, but often the Lord wants to lead us beyond the repetition of a previous level of growth. Progress is dependent on seeing the Lord's vision and allowing him to define the steps to reach it. He gives an anointing for that.

I long for the anointing for the responsibilities God has given me. I know when it happens. When I am writing there are times my pen is given wings and I am able to write insights beyond my training and skill. When I study a passage in preparation for preaching or writing, there is a blessed time when suddenly the Scripture yields its deepest secrets. The anointing is given. There are times when I'm preaching that the electric moment happens. All the study and manuscripting is only preparation for that anointed time when words are given life, and profound communication between people and preacher is given. Often, I am given a fresh insight which is God's particular word to someone he has brought to church for that special arrow of truth. People leave church saying, "How did you know I needed that?" I didn't, but the Anointer did. In counseling, I have learned also that while I listen the Lord often gives a sacred moment of insight which is his liberating key to unlock the future for a person. It was a gift. The Lord's anointing made possible a wisdom beyond my own insight.

We should not be surprised when this happens. Jesus promised that we could expect the anointing in life's tight places. He told the disciples that they would be given supernatural power to speak and act in each new situation. "Do not be anxious how or what you are to answer or what you are to say; for the Holy Spirit will teach you in that very hour what you ought to say" (Luke 12:11–12). This is the source of true freedom. It flows from abiding in Christ. He is never inadequate for any situation we face. An anointing for today's pressures is just a prayer away.

My observation of Christians who have experienced anointing is that it gives them a warmth and viability. The abiding

Christ shines through. Defensiveness is gone; dependence gives joy. They have an attractive winsomeness which is communicated.

A *chrisma* must precede charisma: an anointing is the prelude to receiving the grace gifts we need for our responsibilities and relationships.

The other day, a woman asked, "Are you charismatic?" My response was, "Spell that, please!" Surprised, she spelled, "C-h-a-r-i-s-m-a-t-i-c." The extra letter *a* makes the difference. In the Greek, however, there's a real distinction. *Charisma* means grace-gifted. The word comes from *charismata,* grace gift; *charis*-grace; *mata*-gift.

In 1 Corinthians 12:4, Paul speaks of the diversities of gifts, *charismatōn.* Our word *charisma* is rooted in this idea. A charismatic person is one who is given the gifts of the Holy Spirit for his ministry. The confusion about the term has arisen from those who claim that the gift of tongues is the only undeniable outward evidence of the indwelling of the Holy Spirit. The Lord wants to give us all the gifts delineated in 1 Corinthians 12 and Romans 12. No one of the gifts is the sure sign of charisma. We need wisdom, knowledge, faith, healing, miracles, prophesy, and discernment as well as the gift of tongues.

Leave the addition of the *a* up to the Lord. We are to seek, pray, and open ourselves to the *chrisma*; the charisma which results will be the Lord's doing. Charisma is inadvertent and flows from the *chrisma*. Without an anointing we are destined to a life of stress and strain. It makes all the difference if we can expect and joyously receive the Lord's anointing in the excruciating demands of life. A *chrisma* is the first step to everywhere!

PRAYER FOR THE DAY: *Lord, you know better than I what's ahead. Go before me to show the way. Then meet me in each person and situation. Anoint me with your Holy Spirit so that I will know what to say and do. Help me to anticipate and enjoy your intervention. Here are my mind, will, and voice. Thank you for your abiding presence and power. Give me the freedom and joy of knowing that your special anointing will give me exactly what I need. Thank you for liberating me from the necessity of being adequate on my own. In the name of Christ, I accept your chrisma, the only source of authentic charisma. Amen.*

10.

God Can Make You Wise

His anointing teaches you about everything.

1 John 2:27

READ: 1 John 2:26–27

As both friend and counselor, I try to listen to people carefully with an outer and inner ear—with one to hear what they are saying; the other to hear what God may be saying to them. My purpose is not to give advice, but to help a person to clarify a problem or opportunity, and then to receive God's strategy for the next steps.

We all have decisions to make. The alternatives are often beguiling and confusing. We must make evaluations of people and their potential. All of us urgently need guidance for our long-and short-range goals. Most of all, we need penetrating vision into God's plan for our lives.

My constant prayer for myself and other people is for wisdom. And God is not reluctant to respond. Often, he is more ready to give the gift than we are to ask.

The anointing of the Holy Spirit enables wisdom. More than human sagacity, wisdom is what is given when all our in-

72

tellectual and intuitive faculties are under the control of the abiding, indwelling Lord. He gives us the capacity to plumb the depths of the nature of God, discover his purposes, and discern his specific will for our direction and daily decisions. The Spirit unveils the mystery of God and heightens our capacity to see what he is doing in the world and how we can cooperate with him.

The practical application of wisdom is discernment. It's wisdom at work. There is no decision so large or difficulty so small that a *chrisma* of the Spirit will not give us what we need to maximize every day of our lives.

John wanted his friends to claim the gift of wisdom which was theirs through the anointing of the Spirit. The Christians had become defensive under the arrogant attacks of the Gnostics. The philosophers claimed to have an esoteric secret wisdom about life and God. The Apostle put it sharply. "I write this to you about those who would deceive you; but the anointing which you received from him abides in you, and you have no need that any one should teach you; as his anointing teaches you about everything, and is true, and is no lie; just as it has taught you, abide in him" (1 John 2:26–27).

The anointing teaches you about everything! Quite a promise! We want to claim it for ourselves in this chapter by looking at the biblical meaning of wisdom. My intention is that we will receive, experience, and employ the wisdom God offers. Wisdom is the crucial hinge on which the gigantic door opens to unleash the flow of God's power in our lives. It enables us to know how to pray, what to do, how to relate to people, and how to grasp the unlimited potential of our years.

If you could ask for one gift from God, apart from love which is ours without asking, what would you ask? That was the question the Lord put to young Solomon in a dream, at the beginning of his rule over Israel. Solomon had gone to Gibeon with an immense challenge before him. He had inherited the kingdom from his father, David. Was he up to the demands? Could he rule with the insight and charisma he had seen in his father? Did he have what it would take? He feared that he did not have the strength and leadership skills both the Lord and Israel needed from him. Trembling with trepidation over the impossibility, Solomon went to the worship site at Gibeon. We are told that he "used to offer a thousand burnt offerings upon that altar" (1 Kings 3:4). That means that the privilege of leadership had driven him to pray to the Lord.

It was while he was there that the Lord made the uncertain king an astounding offer: "Ask what I shall give you."

How would you have answered? We can empathize with Solomon's caution in response. Like the youthful monarch, we too face impossibilities and tasks beyond our strength. Or we should! God never makes that offer until we have assumed a challenge we could not handle on our own resources. He is constantly pressing us on in the adventure of living, into situations we cannot meet, problems we cannot solve, complexities we cannot understand.

What is it for you? Focus in your mind's eye the relationship in which you are being stretched for compassion and understanding, the task which defies resolution, the difficulty which mocks your inadequacy. Now listen to the Lord! "Ask what I shall give you."

Solomon's answer was not glib. He chose his words carefully. The young man had learned the secret of his father's greatness. David was known as a man after God's own heart. That meant he had a heart which was subsequent, similar, in search of, and submissive to the very heart of God. David's intuitive insight came from intense intimacy with God. The Psalmist knew the forgiveness of the love of God and the power of praise to unlocking the potential of God. David was one of the greatest sinners and saints of the Old Testament. He was a man after God's heart in his times of need, and a man whose heart was shaped often in accordance with the grace of God. By his failures as well as his triumphs, David had given his son Solomon the most important gift a father can give: knowledge that the heart of the need is the need of the heart; and that the heart of the matter is who is master of the heart.

And so Solomon told God he wanted a heart like David's. He too wanted to be a man, a king, a leader after God's heart. Listen to his plea: "Give thy servant therefore an understanding heart to judge thy people, that I may discern between good and bad; for who is able to judge this thy so great a people?" (1 Kings 3:9, KJV).

The heart for the Hebrews meant the intellect, emotions, and will. It was the core of a person's being. Solomon wanted his heart of hearts wholly and completely obedient to the will of God so that he could govern wisely and well. The word "understanding" means hearing—a hearing heart. It is used here as the capacity to hear and obey. Solomon wanted to be receptive to all that God had to give.

But the young king did not want a hearing heart for his own enjoyment. He longed to be receptive so that he could discern what was right and do it. In asking for an understanding heart to obey, he was asking for the spiritual gift of wisdom. That God answered his prayer is evident in the fact that wisdom became synonymous with his name. The "wisdom of Solomon" punctuates his time of history.

Wisdom is our greatest need today. We need it for our responsibilities and relationships. It is the missing quality in most leaders, the lacking ingredient in society, the reason for the impotence and ineptness of most Christians.

We worship at the shrine of fact, place our oblations on the altar of knowledge, and bow down before our capacity to solve the mysteries of life. We live as paupers of the mind because we lack the power of wisdom.

True wisdom cannot be earned or acquired by human effort. Nor is it reserved for old age, or the result of experience alone. We can have lived long and squeezed the fruit of life dry and not have wisdom. Wisdom is a gift. It is imparted by

God, imputed in communion with him, and infused by his Holy Spirit. It is beyond acquired skills. Deeper than insight. More profound than learning.

Do you have the gift of wisdom? You can! The first step to greatness, effectiveness, and inner power for living is wisdom. You can receive the gift today. Right now. An understanding heart filled with wisdom can be yours!

Wisdom is synonymous with the creative energies of God. It's another term for the Logos, or Word of God, through whom the Lord created and sustained the universe. Solomon learned this and shared his discovery in his book of wisdom, the Proverbs. "The Lord by wisdom founded the earth, by understanding he established the heavens; by his knowledge the deeps broke forth and the clouds drop down dew" (Prov. 3: 19–20).

That same wisdom called and appointed Israel to be his people. Israel was blessed to be a blessing to all mankind. The great leaders of Israel became the spectacular men and women they were, not because of human skill and sagacity, but because they received the gift of imparted wisdom.

But always it was received in a crisis over the depletion of their own creativity. The cul-de-sac of impossibility drove them back to communion with Yahweh. In response, wisdom was given. Battles were fought, the Exodus accomplished, the Red Sea opened, the promised land claimed, the Kingdom established—all because of people like Abraham, Moses, Gideon, David, and Solomon, who got to the end of themselves and found wisdom waiting.

Solomon put it clearly: "The fear of the Lord is the beginning of wisdom" (Prov. 1:7). Awe and wonder in the face of human inadequacy is the undeniable prelude to wisdom. When we have done all we can, when the facts spell no solution, when our emptiness is confessed, and when the arrogance of self-will is exposed, wisdom is given. Never before.

Job was driven to admit that. "But where shall wisdom be found? And where is the place of understanding? Man does not know the way to it, and it is not found in the land of the living. . . . Whence then comes wisdom? And where is the place of understanding? It is hid from the eyes of all living, and concealed from the birds of the air. Abaddon and Death say, 'We have heard a rumor of it with our ears' " (Job 28: 12–13, 20–22).

Abaddon, the abyss, and death—how would they give a word about wisdom? It is on the boundary line of human existence—at the point of inadequacy, when we face the limitation of our resources—that wisdom is given. As Paul Tillich explains: "There can be no wisdom without an encounter with the holy, with that which creates awe, and shakes the ordinary way of life and thought. Without the experience of awe in the face of the mystery of life, there is no wisdom."

The experience of our finitude is the beginning of wisdom. Then we can face our limitations and we pray for help. You and I are most richly blessed when the crises and challenges of life bring us to the place where we can cry out, "Lord, help me! It's beyond me! I don't know what to do, say, or be." It's the moment of brokenness that leads to the wholeness of wisdom.

The world teetered on the brink of despair at history's lowest ebb, when wisdom became incarnate in Jesus Christ. The eternal Holy God—creator, sustainer, and guiding Lord of history—came in response to a few faithful whose cry was, "O come, O come Immanuel." In Jesus of Nazareth, wisdom dwelt bodily. Luke records the awesome gift: "And the child grew and became strong, filled with wisdom; and the favor of God was upon him" (Luke 2:40). And "Jesus increased in wisdom and in stature, and in favor with God and man" (Luke 2:52). The wisdom of Jesus astonished people wherever he went. "Where did this man get this wisdom and these mighty works?" Where indeed! He was the wisdom of God incarnate. But only the meek and humble received him. "He came to his own home, and his own people received him not. But to all who received him, who believed in his name, he gave power to become the children of God" (John 1:11–12). Those who refused nailed him to the cross. Arrogance, self-satisfaction, pride in religion, and human understanding always do that to wisdom.

But that was not the end of the matter. The early church looked back at the incarnation and realized that the cross was the ultimate revelation of the wisdom of God, and the only source of the experience of wisdom. Paul articulated that in his letter to the Corinthians. "For the word of the cross is folly to those who are perishing, but to us who are being saved it is the power of God. For it is written, 'I will destroy the wisdom of the wise, and the cleverness of the clever I will thwart.' Where is the wise man? Where is the scribe? Where is the debater of this age? Has not God made foolish the wisdom of the world? For since, in the wisdom of God, the world did not know God through wisdom, it pleased God through the folly of what we preach to save those who believe. For Jews demand signs and Greeks seek wisdom, but we preach Christ crucified, a stumbling block to Jews and folly to Gentiles, but to those who are called, both Jews and Greeks, Christ the power of God and the wisdom of God. For the foolishness of God is wiser than men, and the weakness of God is stronger than men" (1 Cor. 1:18–25).

What does that mean to you and me? Just this! It flatly answers Job's question, "Canst thou, by searching, find God?" No!—that's Paul's resounding message—neither by being religious or learned. We cannot work into a knowledge of God. He has come to us. He has told us who he is and the only way we can know him. The cross is the sublime revelation of the previously hidden mystery of his nature of love and forgiveness.

That is a stumbling block to religious people. Our pride is exposed! We cannot earn a status with God. The inclusive love of God, freely offered on the cross for our sins, finally excludes our self-righteousness. How can one who ended up on a cross reveal God to us? We want signs of his power, not suffering. We are brought to the abyss of insufficiency, to the death of our arrogance. We are helpless to be good enough. God makes his presence and power known with irresistible conviction in the act of will by which we surrender without reserve to the Highest we know. We possess wisdom when we become God-possessed. That's when wisdom is given. The cross is foolishness to the intellectual who believes that clear thinking can capture truth about God. All our knowledge cannot solve the riddle of our existence or give us power to live abundantly. The Greeks of old thought of God as all good, and matter as evil. How could a good God assume evil nature in an incarnation? And how could the death of a man on the cross reveal God? Or why does anyone need a Savior if he does not consider himself a sinner? That's the rub. Foolishness indeed! The secret source is still the hearing heart. Humility is the only way. It's the virtue which is born at the foot of the cross.

The cross is not only the final and ultimate revelation of God's heart, it is the prelude to the exposure of his power. The crucifixion is irrevocably followed by the resurrection. Christ's death deals with our sin; the resurrection deals with our impatience.

And now we are at the core of it. The cycle of death and resurrection is the secret of wisdom. The cross is then and now. If it was not then, it cannot be now. But if it is not now as a personal experience, what it was then is robbed of its power for us. The Christian life begins not only with an acceptance of Christ's death for our sins; it is enabled by the death of our own efforts, scheming, manipulation, and self-righteousness. Paul said, "I have been crucified with Christ; it is no longer I who live but Christ who lives in me" (Gal. 2:20). And, "If we have been buried with him in a death like his we shall be raised in a resurrection like his" (Rom. 6:4). That's where it all begins. It is life's greatest crisis: the crucifixion of self, the surrender of our lives, the opening of our hearts. It is then that the resurrected, living Lord makes our hearts his post-resurrection home.

What would you say? Does Christ live in you? He died for you! He was raised up for you! He created your heart—the combination of mind, emotion, and will—for himself. You belong to him! Listen to Paul's word to you, "Christ is the source of your life, whom God made our wisdom . . ." and, "this is the mystery hidden for ages—Christ in you the hope of Glory" (Col. 1:26).

Christ himself, indwelling in us, is the source of our wisdom. Our minds can receive the mind of Christ, our emotions can be infused with his love so that we can be to each other what he has been to us, and our wills can be fired with power to discern and do his will.

We no longer need to muddle through our decisions. We can receive the precious gift of wisdom which will give us our Lord's perspective on all our uncertainties and complexities.

Catch Paul's excitement about that. "We impart a secret and hidden wisdom of God, which God decreed before the ages for our glorification" (1 Cor. 2:7). "God has revealed to us through the spirit. For the Spirit searches everything, even the depths of God. For what person knows a man's thoughts except the spirit of the man which is in him? So also no one comprehends the thoughts of God except the Spirit of God. Now we have received the . . . Spirit which is from God, that we might understand the gifts bestowed on us by God. And we impart this in words not taught by human wisdom but taught by the Spirit, interpreting spiritual truths to those who possess the Spirit. . . . We have the mind of Christ" (1 Cor. 2:10–13; 16).

Now problems become the source of new possibilities. Paul reaches the height of his crescendo when he affirms that all things are ours. "For all things are yours . . . the world or life or death or the present or the future, all are yours; and you are Christ's and Christ is God's" (1 Cor. 3:21–23).

Wisdom is the first of the gifts given to a hearing heart. In the list of the gifts of the Holy Spirit, the indwelling Christ in

1 Corinthians 12, wisdom is first and primary. Paul calls it the gift of the "utterance of wisdom."

This is how it works. When we open ourselves to the Holy Spirit and ask for clarity, discernment, and insight into people, problems, and perplexities, we are given supernatural wisdom to know what to do and what to say. We will know how to solve problems, how to speak in a given situation, and how to move through the tangled maze of human opinions and alternatives. The gift of the utterance of wisdom is first spoken by the Spirit to our hearing hearts before we speak it to others. That means prolonged prayer. "Lord, here is my heart! What do you want me to do or say? What is your wisdom which will help me break through this uncertainty?"

I remember a time in my life when I was depleted emotionally and intellectually from the challenges I faced. I'll never forget stumbling over Christ's word, "Apart from me you can do nothing." I prayed, "Lord, I don't want to try to make it any longer without you"—the abyss of helplessness and the death of self-effort. When I returned to my work, I was refreshed. But more than that, I sensed a new capacity to penetrate problems, see with x-ray vision beneath the surface of people, and incisively speak the truth I had received as a gift from the Lord.

The most exciting thing I see happening in our time is the liberation of a whole new breed of laity, people who have been given the gift of wisdom for their personal and professional responsibilities.

I talked to a famous cancer surgeon in Houston, Texas, the other day. "We are on the edge of a momentous new breakthrough in the cure of cancer. But I know it will not be a result of scientific effort alone. The Lord is giving us the secret we have searched for so long." This man's recent commitment to Christ has opened him to the possibility of wisdom which exceeds his immense learning and skill.

I met with a group of executives who are responsible for

large corporate management. They meet together consistently to seek the Lord's wisdom.

I talked to a prominent judge who takes the excruciatingly painful decisions to the Lord in prayer, asking for divine wisdom. He attests to frequent interventions from the Lord which have given him the wisdom he's needed.

The other day I sat down with a leading educator. He was facing the challenge of how to build a university which would equip leaders for the complexities of our time. He said he had taken a long period away from his responsibilities to think and pray. He asked God for the one-, three-, and five-year goals for his university. In the quiet, he received wisdom to see the future strategy unfold. And it's happening the way the Lord told him it would!

I've talked to parents who have asked for wisdom and have been amazed at the new insight and discernment they had for their families.

I know of a psychiatrist who prays all through his counseling, asking for penetrating sensitivity and empathy. He affirms that it's while he prays and listens that thoughts come which are the key to healing a troubled person.

There is a sacred moment in every research, problem-solving effort, or search for direction. It comes after we have done our homework, gathered the facts, and done our best. It is the moment of the grand "Aha!" Suddenly things fall into place. An aside, a seemingly insignificant fact we had by-passed, a previously undiscovered insight, and we say, "Aha! Why had I never thought of that?" The gift of wisdom has been given.

James says, "If any of you lacks wisdom, let him ask God, who gives to all men generously and without reproaching, and it will be given him" (James 1:5). God is more ready to give wisdom than we are to ask. James also speaks of the meekness of wisdom (3:13). There's the condition of humility again! The word *meekness* implies the willingness to be led. The Greek word for meek, *praus,* is used for an animal which has been domesticated and trained to obey the command and the

touch of the reins of its master. The Greeks also used the word
meek for the opposite of *hupsēlokardia,* which means lofty-
heartedness or arrogant resistance to be taught. Without a
realization of our ignorance there can be no learning. Quinti-
lian, the great Roman orator, said of his students, "They
would no doubt be excellent students if they were not already
convinced of their own knowledge." Meekness is the humility
of knowing we need forgiveness, the cross, and the gift of wisdom from the indwelling Lord of our hearts. And the Lord's
promise is sure and irrevocable: "Blessed are the meek, for
they shall inherit the earth."

We have come full circle back to Solomon's prayer for an
understanding heart. A hearing heart. A receptive heart. A
Spirit-filled heart. A heart of wisdom. Is that what you'd ask
of God if he gave you one wish?

John would want us to know that wisdom is not ours just for
the asking. It's ours for the using. Wisdom has already been
given. The issue is our anointing. If we have accepted the
anointing of the Lord, he abides in us. Our prayer then is,
"Lord, thank you for abiding in me. I know I belong to you
and that all my days are in your hands. Help me to appropriate the wisdom you have given me. Use my intellect and intui-
tion to know and do your will."

We can move into our challenges today knowing that the
gift of wisdom will be given. We can anticipate and graciously
accept that God will make us wise!

PRAYER FOR THE DAY: *Infinite Wisdom, you know how much
we need the perspective of your plan and purpose for us
today. In our responsibilities and relationships we must
make decisions and crucial evaluations. Our lives, and the
people we love, are dependent on the wisdom we receive from
you. Give us the Apostle John's confident assurance that we
have been anointed and that, therefore, your wisdom is available. We need the humility to claim what is ours, and the au-*

dacity to follow the guidance you give. Thank you for mak-
ing us wise today. In the name of the one who was Incarnate
Wisdom and abides in us. Amen.

11.

Can You Imagine?—
Assurance and Aspiration

Beloved, we are God's children now; it does not yet appear what we shall be, but we know that when he appears we shall be like him.

1 John 3:2

READ: 1 John 3:1–3

I once had a parishioner whose constant response in conversation was, "Can you imagine." People were never sure whether there was a question mark or an exclamation point after her compulsive comment. Whatever you said to Blanche, whether it was about the mundane or the momentous, you could be sure she would punctuate it with, "Well, can you imagine!?"

She meant well, but it agitated people, especially her husband. I felt him cringe every time she blurted it out. One evening while visiting in their home, I sensed her husband's patience had run out. She said it once too often. His rapier reply was, "Yes, Blanche, I can imagine and let me tell you what I imagine: what life would be like without you constantly saying 'Can you imagine'!"

Blanche's conversational tick makes us laugh, but her question needs to be asked. Can you imagine?

Recently, I was startled by a giant billboard. In bold letters it posed another question. "If you had to lose one of your faculties, what would you miss the most?" I pondered that long and hard as I drove along the crowded freeway. How would you have answered? Sight? Smell? Hearing? I thought about being without any of them. You'll be happy to know that I didn't close my eyes while driving to experience what it would be like to be blind!

Two things competed for first place of what I would want least to lose—memory and imagination. They are both part of the capacity to think. But thinking without either would be dull and bland. Then I came to the conclusion that memory and imagination are inseparably related. What we dare to imagine is based on the memory of fulfilled imaginings of the past. Assurance enables aspiration.

John wanted his friends to discover the gift of imagination to picture what they could become. He touches all three dimensions of time. In retrospect, they could see what God had done for them. "See what love the Father has given us, that we should be called children of God." The present was therefore filled with confident assurance. "And so we are. Beloved, we are God's children now." On the basis of that, they could have hope for the future. "It does not yet appear what we shall be, but we know that when he appears, we shall be like him, for we shall see him as he is."

Now the secret power of imagination is suggested. "And everyone who thus hopes in him purifies himself as he is pure." Imagination purifies our purpose. It centers our attention on Christ and our hope of becoming like him. Lesser goals are purged. Kierkegaard told us that purity of heart is to will one thing. A Christian, according to John, purifies himself in progressive movement toward Christ and Christlikeness. Impurities of conflicting loyalties are drained off like dross when we center our eyes on Jesus. The unique capacity of imagination is to make us like Christ in thought, action, and reaction. Let's unwrap the special gift God has given us.

Consider first that the gift of imagination is the point of contact with the Holy Spirit.

Remember the conversation between Joan of Arc and Robert de Beaudricourt in George Bernard Shaw's *St. Joan?*

JOAN: "You must not talk to us about my voices."
ROBERT: "How do you mean, voices?"
JOAN: "I hear voices telling me what to do.
          They come from God."
ROBERT: "They come from your imagination!"
JOAN: "Of course. That's how the messages of God come to us."

Indeed! The creative God of all makes us recipients of grace and adventurers in his plans for us and his world. The capacity to form, hold, and achieve mental images is the God-given gift of imagination. An encounter with the living God results in the reformation of our image. It was with imagination that he created us in his own image. Through the ages he mediated to man's minds what he intended his people to be. When he came incarnate as Jesus of Nazareth he gave us the image of what he is like and what we were meant to be. The Apostle Paul pondered that and said, "He is the image of the invisible God" (Col. 1:15). "For in him all the fulness of God was pleased to dwell, and through him to reconcile to himself all things, whether on earth or in heaven, making peace by the blood of his cross" (Col. 1:19–20).

The Christian life begins when we imagine ourselves as loved and forgiven, accepted and affirmed, released and empowered. Christ is our image. The more he is the focus of our imagination, the more we become like him. Knowing what he has done for us, we know what we are to do. We are all in the process of becoming what we envision.

Secondly, the gift of imagination is the bridge over the interface of our presuppositions and our possibilities. Our imagination is God's instrument for actuating our experience of

him and doing his will. It is the servant of the intellect and the
motivator of the will. It is when our knowledge of God and
what he has done is wedded to our imagination that the greatest power for creativity is born. Imagination is the channel of
God's answer to the question, "Now that I believe, what am I
to be and do?" Inspiration becomes specific through the gift
of imagination.

What Shakespeare said of the poet, I say of the Christian:

> The poet's eye, in a fine frenzy rolling,
> Doth glance from heaven to earth, from earth to
>   heaven;
> And, as imagination bodies forth
> The forms of things unknown, the poet's pen
> Turns them to shapes, and gives to airy nothings
> A local habitation and a name.

—*A Midsummer Night's Dream*, 5.1.12–18

Christian discipleship is giving spiritual truth a local habi-
tation and a name. The Spirit invades our imagination to etch
the guidelines of our obedience. He forms an image in our
brains of what we would be like, what we would be with others, and what we would do in society if we trusted him completely. Isn't that magnificent? Can you imagine?

Roger Babson was right. "The future has a habit of becoming the present." That's why John urges us to fix our hope on
Christ. Charles Kettering said, "I expect to spend the rest of
my life in the future, so I want to be reasonably sure of what
kind of future it's going to be. That's my reason for planning."
Imagination is the draftsman of that planning. Some people
say that the future is purchased by the present. John would
tell us that what we experience in the present is dependent on
what we envision for the future.

That leads me to a third thought about Holy Spirit-
inspired imagination. It's the gift to believe the impossible in

the midst of change and difficult circumstances. The prophets of doom constantly compete for the focus of our imagination. The capacity of imagination is neutral. It can reflect negative presuppositions as vividly as God's positive vision.

Negative images besieged the imaginations of the early Christians to whom John wrote. The philosophies of the Gnostics contradicted the incarnation at every turn. Not only did they deny that Jesus was the Son of God, but they insistently taught that he neither lived in the flesh nor died on the cross. A Christian imagination without a clear, vivid belief in the cross is impotent. If Christ did not die for our sins and rise again, what hope do we have for facing our anxieties and frustrations? The beguiling distortion John's reader faced was that God was not concerned or involved in the sorted problems of humanity. The result was the temptation to expect too little from God. John was blunt in his retort: "The reason the world does not know us is that it did not know him."

We face the same problem. It's difficult to have a Spirit-inspired imagination with people around us who have little vision about what God is able to do. Changes and choices can equal collapse or creativity. The only constant in life is change. Change is life. Our choices in response to those changes determine our tomorrows. Henry T. Kaiser used to say that when a tough, challenging job had to be done, he looked for a person who possessed an enthusiasm and optimism for life, who made a zestful, confident attack on his daily problems, one who pinned down his buoyant spirit with careful planning and vibrant hope. We are to be that kind of person for each other.

One of the most inspiring senior church officers I have is Robert Hicks. He has helped hundreds of people recapture the power of imagination. As a psychologist he has led his patients in discovering the person God meant them to be and in daring to picture what they could become.

Early in my Hollywood ministry, Dr. Hicks sent me a poem

by an anonymous author which has been a source of rekindled imagination:

All Things Possible

Filled with a strange new hope they came,
The blind, the leper, the sick, the lame.
Frail of body and spent of soul . . .
As many as touched Him were made whole.

On every tongue was the Healer's name,
Through all the country they spread His fame.
But *doubt* clung tight to his wooden crutch
Saying, "*We must not expect too much.*"

Down through the ages a promise came,
Healing for sorrow and sin and shame,
Help for the helpless and sight for the blind,
Healing for body and soul and mind.

The Christ we follow is still the same,
With blessings that all who will may claim.
But how often we miss Love's healing touch
By thinking, "*We must not expect too much.*"

Leo Tolstoy said that familiarity is the opiate of the imagination. That's what lulls us into expecting too little from God and therefore attempting too little for God. What James Weldon Johnson prayed for the preacher in "Listen Lord," I pray for you and me:

Put his eye to the telescope of eternity,
And let him look upon the paper thin walls of time.
Lord, turpentine his imagination,
Fill him full of the dynamic of thy power,
Anoint him all over with the oil of thy salvation,
And set his tongue on fire.

Lastly, imagination enables the capacity to believe that the best is still to be. Do you believe that the most exciting time of your life is ahead of you? That's the sure test of an imaginative Christian. We can live in the viability of John's confidence that "it does not yet appear what we shall be." Not to worry! We will see more of Christ in whatever happens to us and he will use everything to make us more like himself. The resurrection is the source of our confidence. The empty tomb is our symbol that if God raised Jesus from the dead, he will invade all our tomorrows with unexpected interventions. Dorothy Sayers said it with her irrepressible gusto. "The resurrection has caused the world to palpitate with new possibilities." And our liberated, Spirit-filled, unvarnished imaginations will grasp those possibilities.

That's your cue, Blanche. "Can you imagine!?"

Well, can we?

A GUIDE FOR THE CREATIVE USE OF IMAGINATION IN PRAYER:

- Creative listening is the essence of prayer.
- Focus your entire attention on God.
- Relax your body. Free your emotions to respond.
- Review in your mind who he is.
- Say the words which describe his nature.
- Thank him for what he has revealed of himself in Jesus.
- Repeat the name of Jesus as you remember his birth, life, message, death, resurrection, return in power at Pentecost.
- Allow your heart to soar in adoration.
- Now confess your sins. Sin is anything which stands between you and him or between you and any other human being. What you have done or failed to do. Tell him *all* about it.
- Thank him for his forgiveness. Picture yourself at the foot of the cross looking at him suffer for you! Amazing grace! Gratitude.
- Now spread out all your needs before him. Ask him to talk to you about what he wants you to be and do.

- What are the specific things he tells you? Write them down! Ponder them. Commit yourself to obey.
- Ask God to coat your imagination with turpentine and remove the layers of varnished reserve.
- Next walk into your future. Picture yourself filled with the joy, love, and courage of Christ. Thank him for the vision he gives your imagination for the future in the image of Christ.
- Finally, surrender as much as you now know of yourself to as much as you have seen of the person your sanctified imagination has pictured.

12.

Superseding the Syndrome

No one born of God commits sin; for God's nature abides in him.

1 John 3:9

READ: 1 John 3:4–10

A new Christian came to see me about a problem of discouragement. He told me that when he committed his life to Christ, he expected to be completely different. The possibility of becoming a new person in Christ had attracted him. The person who had helped him become a Christian had promised him an instant change in his life. He had heard about the miraculous transformations which had taken place in other people's lives. The man expected nothing less for himself.

"When I surrendered my life to Christ," he said, "I felt an immediate joy and excitement. The Lord's forgiveness helped me deal with my past failures and sins. I felt loved and accepted. The delight of my new-found relationship has lasted and grown until last week. Then I crashed! The emotional excitement drained out of me."

Having heard statements like that hundreds of times, I began to probe to find the reason for the man's diminished joy. I was not surprised when he told me that he had blown it in a very crucial relationship in his family. "I acted like I used to before I became a Christian. I said and did things I thought I would never say and do again. Maybe I didn't really become a Christian. How could I have done that if I have Christ? Why does it take so long to grow up as a Christian?"

Sound familiar? Ever felt like that? We all have. Most of us are alarmed at what we do, believing all that we do about what a Christian life should be. Our daily failures make us question our commitment. That leads to the false assumption that if we had more faith we would have a final breakthrough to permanent perfection.

When we read John's letter we realize that the problem of Christian growth has been around a long time. At first reading, there seems to be a contradiction in John's admonitions. We are comforted by some and disturbed by others. In the first chapter we are challenged to admit and confess our sins. "If we say we have no sin, we deceive ourselves, and the truth is not in us. If we confess our sins, he is faithful and just, and will forgive our sins and cleanse us from all unrighteousness. If we say we have not sinned, we make him a liar and his word is not in us" (1 John 1:8–10). That's a comforting assurance. We are like those early Christians. We, too, know the problem of failure after we become Christians. Perhaps we are not so bad after all. There will always be a distance between what we believe and how completely we are able to live out Christ's love in our relationships.

But then we read 1 John 3:4–10. We wonder if this was written by the same author. It seems to be diametrically contrary to what he has said previously. More than that, John makes a demand on us that we know we can't live up to. Self-doubt settles in. Who can reach the level of perfection suggested here? What do you make of this?

"You know," says John, "that he [Christ] appeared to take away sins, and in him there is no sin. No one who abides in him sins; no one who sins has either seen him or known him.

Little children, let no one deceive you. He who does right is righteous, as he is righteous. He who commits sin is of the devil; for the devil has sinned from the beginning. The reason the Son of God appeared was to destroy the works of the devil. No one born of God commits sin; for God's nature abides in him, and he cannot sin because he is from God" (1 John 3: 5–9). That blows any cool assurance! At first we feel condemned and then frustrated by the impossibility of the Apostle's seemingly rigid requirement. We want to be honest. We all know that since we began the Christian life, we have sinned. In fact, many of us have grown as we have acknowledged our sins and allowed Christ to love us afresh. So what are we going to do with this portion of scripture?

We must plunge deeper into what John meant. The two portions of his letter are actually two parts of a central truth. The first two verses in chapter 2 are a bridge over the two seemingly contradictory messages. Here's the key to unlock the mystery: "My little children, I am writing this to you so that you may not sin; but if anyone does sin, we have an advocate with the Father, Jesus Christ the righteous; and he is the expiation for our sins, and not for ours only but also for the sins of the whole world." Whew! Things may not be as grim as we thought!

The Greek verb form of the injunction not to sin is important here. It is in the aorist tense, indicating a specific, definite, and particular act of sin. We are encouraged not to do these singular sins of thought or action. But when we do, we have Christ to stand beside us to help us confess what has happened and to assure us of forgiveness. We all sin—miserably and often. Fresh atonement is but a prayer away. And then the realization dawns on us: the more we are forgiven, the less we want to do these individual acts of rebellion.

In the passage from the third chapter, a different tense is used for the verb *to sin*. Note verse 9 in particular. The verb is in the linear present active indicative tense, meaning constant, consistent, and compulsive action. This is the kind of sin from which we have been liberated. We have been set free of habitual sin as the dominant desire of our lives. We will know temporary lapses, but our conversion has meant a dramatic demarcation, a turning around. We have turned from a life directed away from God to a life moving closer and closer to him. Our passion is now to glorify God and enjoy him in all things. There may be separate acts which alarm us and show that we are still clay being molded, but the Father's hand is persistently shaping us in the image of Christ.

My new Christian friend was a good example of the two verb forms John uses. He had committed an *aorist* kind of sin. It did not mean that his new life was up for grabs. It was up for grace. The basic intention of his mind and heart was to love as he had been loved by the Savior. His failure in this instance simply helped him to see that he was a person in process. The sure sign that Christ had taken hold of his life was that he could recognize what he had done and desire forgiveness. He was experiencing spiritual growing pains. What he would never have given a second thought to before or would have justified defensively, he now could see as a contradiction of his basic purpose of being a communicator of love. Like Paul, he could forget what was behind because it had been forgiven, and press on to the upward call of God.

John was not trying to teach a negative perfectionism. He was confronting the pious perfectionism of some of the Gnostics who claimed that their esoteric insight made them sinless and perfect. With a play on Greek tenses, John exposed their false assumption. It was the Christians who had been liberated from the incarceration of habitual, compulsive sin.

Let's follow the Apostle's thought further. He says anyone "born of God" is no longer under the control of Satan and the insidious influence to resist and rebel. The reason is made clear: "No one born of God commits sin; for God's nature abides in him, and he cannot sin because he is born of God."

The words "born of God" and "God's nature abides" hold

powerful potential for our growth as Christians. Here's the source of our hope of sinning less and less. The Greek words again give us clarity. God's seed, *sperma*, has been implanted in us. The divine principle of true life has been given for the conception of the new person inside us. And just as a natural child grows to have the characteristics of the impregnating father, so too we increasingly grow in our Heavenly Father's spiritual nature. The word *nature* means disposition and temperament. Once the seed is planted, the fetus of new life begins to grow. When we believe, the new person is born and begins to replace the old nature with its attitudes, disposition, and temperament. We become more and more like Christ. This is the meaning of Paul's admonition, "Have this mind among yourselves" (Phil. 2:5). The word *mind* in this case also means disposition or nature. Another way of translating what Paul said would be, "Have Christ's disposition for one another." And that process goes on all through our lives. The Lord is never finished with us. His nature continues to captivate and pervade our old nature.

That's the antidote to sin. The more we concentrate on Christ, the more we will desire to be like him and do what he would do in each situation and relationship.

I meet defeated Christians everywhere. They are living on self-effort, trying to be adequate and perfect on their own strength. The great need is to abide in Christ and for him to abide in them. The first is the best we can do, and the second is the best he can offer. Abiding in Christ is concentrating our total experience on him. It's energetic, intellectual contemplation of Christ and the implications of the incarnation. We all need to think a great deal more about Christ. That releases emotions of love and praise. Willingness to do his will follows naturally. We all become what we think about during the waking hours of our day.

But focusing on Christ is only the beginning. Liberating power comes from the indwelling Christ abiding in us. From within he enables us to think his thoughts, express his love, and will to follow his guidance. Extraordinary wisdom, strength, sensitivity, courage, and vision are given to multiply our human capacities. The same passionate obedience to God which we observe in Jesus during his ministry is engendered in us as the urgent desire of our lives. What the Lord requires he releases within us as a gift.

We can supersede the syndrome. The Lord breaks the bind of the cycle of repeated failures. The signs of abnormality of the syndrome become less evident as we habitually focus on Christ. We don't have to stay the way we are. The Lord's nature is growing in us. Ours is to choose to give him complete freedom to dominate our desires. The transformation of personality is a miracle, and we are to be the Lord's miracle in the midst of a world longing for power to live life to the fullest.

John's focus of sin in this passage deals with relationships. Sin is refusal to love. Specific acts of sin are what we do to hurt or debilitate people. But each time we fail, we are called back to our essential purpose of becoming lovers. And the Lord is always more ready to help than we are to ask.

PRAYER FOR THE DAY: *Lord, your patience with us is a source of amazement and contrition. You accept us as we are, but you never leave us there. Thank you for implanting your nature within us so that, as "born of God" Christians, we can joyously anticipate that you will make us like Christ in our disposition, temperament, and attitudes. You know that we do not want to sin. Thank you for forgiving any temporary aberrations. Enable us to accept your forgiveness and move on to growing up in Christ. In this time of conversation with you, we consciously confess our dominant desire to love and obey you. We know that nothing can separate us from you now. It may seem that we have let go of you at times; thank you for never letting go of us. In the name of Christ, our true nature. Amen.*

13.

The Murderous Absence of Love

Any one who hates his brother is a murderer, and you know that no murderer has eternal life abiding in him.

1 John 3:15

READ: 1 John 3:11–18

Lack of love is murderous. That's the shocking thrust of this section of John's letter. We can imagine the alarm this passage caused in the churches when the Apostle's letter was read to the Christians. He wanted to startle them with the urgency of loving.

The challenge to love one another is repeated so often in Christian fellowship and worship today that we no longer hear it. We need to read John's disturbing words with more than "ho-hum" familiarity. He shakes us with the realization that absence of love for people may be contributing to their emotional and spiritual demise.

The walking dead, love-starved people—I meet them everywhere. Young, old, rich, poor. Many of them come from Christian families. Some are married to Christians. Most of them are members of Christian churches. And yet, their deepest need is for a profound experience of human love.

God has called us to be lovers. He came in Jesus Christ to love us so we would be liberated to love as we've been loved. His death on the cross is our motive and mission. God meets the aching need for love he created in people by loving us and enabling us to be human channels of his love to each other. Life is incomplete without his healing love through Christ, and human love from one another. "For this is the message which we have heard from the beginning, that we should love one another." The message never changes. It is the irreducible requirement of being a new person in Christ. Why, then, is it difficult for us to love? We know how much we need divine and human love, ourselves. What keeps us from giving what we need so desperately?

John answers our question by reminding us of Cain and Abel. We are not to be "like Cain, who was of the evil one and murdered his brother. Why did he murder him? Because his own deeds were evil and his brother's righteous." Cain was not satisfied with the Lord's response to his offering. Genesis tells us that he became angry and his countenance fell. Here is a classic case of anger, bitterness, and contempt, as the result of insecurity with the Lord. Cain had not heard God's reassurance of his particularized love for him when God said, "Why are you angry, and why has your countenance fallen? If you do well, will you not be accepted?" Jealousy and competitive hostility resulted in Cain's murdering his brother, Abel.

The most haunting question in Scripture is asked by God after the tragic fratricide. "Where is Abel your brother?" Cain's answer was in another question that has echoed through the ages. "I do not know; am I my brother's keeper?"

We wonder why John used as violent an example as this one from the Old Testament to drive home the urgency of loving. Perhaps it was because he saw the same seeds of destruction in people as were in Cain of old. Lack of love between Christians in the church was caused by the same insecurity with God. Because they would not allow God to love them adequately, they did not love each other sufficiently. We can murder a person's spirit by withholding love. The cause is always a lack of self-love rooted in God's love for us.

John forces us to confront the duality of our natures. We can believe in Christ as our Savior and Lord, participate in the church and pray our prayers, and at the same time be psychologically incapable of being loved or loving. Many of us come to maturity with the scars of childhood on our psyches. An intellectual acceptance of a conceptual faith does not readily change that. Some of us have been deeply hurt in the growing years. Rejection makes us cautious, introverted, or lacking in self-esteem. We expect people to act the same way in our adult years, and we are usually not disappointed. Parents who were starved for human love in childhood inadvertently repeat the pattern. Mates in marriage love each other on the basis of how deeply they were loved in their families.

One afternoon, while counseling, I met with one person after another who was either victim or victimizer because of the lack of healing human love. The frightening thing about that afternoon was that all of the people I talked to were highly educated, cultured Christians who had been raised in Christian families and were part of a Christian church. Most all of the problems could be traced back to emotional malnutrition: broken marriages, family problems, adultery, insecurity, fear, twisted relationships, potential suicide. All in one afternoon! At the end of the exhausting day, I reflected on the causes of the hurt in these people. Each one could verbalize the fact that God loved him, but the psychological need for human love was making them sick, emotional spastics. The unrest I felt put me in touch with what John must have been feeling when he wrote this passage we're considering. The other half of God's love was lacking in the churches to which he wrote: person-to-person love flowing from God's love. How could John get through to the Christians that to be in Christ meant warm, affectionate, affirming love for each other?

Having told them that absence of love was murderous, John

went on with further shock treatment. The evidence that we belong to Christ and are alive forever is that we express healing love to others. "We know that we have passed out of death into life, because we love the brethren. He who does not love abides in death."

That presses you and me back into dialogue. How do you react to John's cutting, incisive message? I must tell you that writing this chapter has been unnerving for me. It's forced me to evaluate my capacity to transmit God's love for me to the people in my life. That prompted me to put into focus the faces of the people who need a human incarnation of God's love. Many of them are fellow Christians who struggle with life because they need to feel that they are important to me, that I have time and affection for them, and that I accept and understand them. I'm learning to take no one for granted. A little boy or girl is inside some of the seemingly "put-together" people. The people who work around and for me need specific expressions of the fact that I value and cherish them. Friends and acquaintances signal the need for me to listen and care profoundly.

How can I touch all the needs of so many people? Ever feel that way? We can't meet people's needs unless we are filled with love from God and significant others in our lives. I find that I need consistent experiences of abiding in prayer to renew my own experience of God's amazing love for me. Added to that, God constantly replenishes me with human love from my wife, family, and a circle of trusted, Spirit-equipped people who are agents of creative, soul-satisfying love from our Lord. My experience in my "church in miniature" sets me free to be a lover. There is no way to meet the demands of people without constantly putting myself in a position to be loved and let people love me.

When I realize how much I need this beloved community, I am renewed in my desire to enable the local church to be a center of love. I talk to clergy all over the country who share my concern. Many of them have realized their own need to experience emotional healing in order to become personified warmth and acceptance in their churches, many of which have become cold religious institutions. I am delighted by the growing number of clergy and church officers who have acknowledged their need to love each other so they can be loving leaders of the congregation. Many are finding that the small group is the answer for the love-starved Christians who populate our churches. Little clusters of people meeting together for Bible study, sharing of needs, and prayer are bringing new warmth to congregations as a whole. I talked to a man recently who has found strength to face life's battles because of the affirming love of a group of businessmen who meet once a week to encourage and pray for each other.

That leads me to John's practical prescription for meeting the love needs in people. He goes beyond shocking admonitions about the lack of love, to show us what to do about it. Remember that his advice was to Christians in the church. "By this we know love, that he laid down his life for us; and we ought to lay down our lives for the brethren."

How can we lay down our lives for fellow Christians? It means involvement, caring, and openness. Loving means listening. People need to articulate their struggles. They long to be drawn out by someone who can understand and probe with identifying tenderness. We lay down our lives by sharing what we've been through or are facing right now. That means sacrificing our personal privacy and images of adequacy. We lock people in a prison of self-doubt if we create the impression we have it all together. No one has! When we dare to be vulnerable, we earn the right to share the answers we have found and to witness to what the Lord has done in our own lives.

Caring for people takes time, surrender of our schedules, and relinquishment of aloof judgmentalism. We will communicate on our faces and in our attitudes whether we are available to care. We all need positive, supportive brothers and sisters in the family of faith to reverse the negative influence of people who have stifled our capacity to give and receive love.

There is no more exciting vocation for a Christian than to be a liberator of people through divinely inspired human expressions of love.

Loving may demand very specific expressions of material help. John presses on to that. "But if any one has the world's goods and sees his brother in need, yet closes his heart against him, how does God's love abide in him? Little children, let us not love in word or speech but in deed and in truth."

The point is that some people cannot hear our words of love until that love is expressed in a way that convinces them we understand what they are going through. An act of love opens people's hearts to hear our words of love. Refocus on the people who need your love. What is the unique and personalized thing you could do to help them in their situations? The Lord is motivating us to act. To refuse the opportunity will debilitate future communication. I know what I must do. How about you?

The Apostle's soaring rhetoric about love has come down to where we live. The words about love bite with impelling necessity to act. It's a life or death matter for people around us. We can enable new life, or we can murder people slowly with the absence of love.

PRAYER FOR THE DAY: *Lord God of love, we thank you for shocking us with the urgency of loving. You created us so that we could not be fulfilled without your love and the love you inspire for us in others. Help us to know what it will mean to lay down our lives for the people around us. Then motivate us to action, so that when this day ends we will be able to feel the excitement of praise for the ways you have loved through us. In the name of Christ our Lord. Amen.*

14.

Have a Heart—For Yourself

By this we shall know that we are of the truth, and assure our hearts before him, whenever our hearts condemn us, for God is greater than our hearts.

1 John 3:19–20

READ: 1 John 3:19–24

"Have a heart!" is a familiar expression when we need a person's understanding, sympathy, or compassion. That's based on a grand assumption. How can we be sure that a person's heart is filled with those qualities?

We think of the heart as the center of feelings. But what's in our hearts depends on what's on our minds. The values, beliefs, and convictions of a person's mind control what's expressed by the heart. It would be well to find out what a person thinks before we plead for him to "have a heart." The mind is the "control center" for what's sent to the nervous system and emotions. The Hebrew understanding of the heart included intellect, emotion, and will. The attitude of the heart is rooted in our beliefs. We'd better check that out when we want someone to "have a heart" for us.

The same is true for our attitudes toward ourselves. We are endowed with the sublime, and sometimes troublesome, capacity of self-evaluation and scrutiny. The great need for most of us is to have a heart for the unique person who lives inside us.

Many of us suffer from a lack of self-affirmation. Life has conditioned us to be very hard on ourselves. We are more aware of our liabilities than our assets. Past failures haunt us and rob us of the delight of the present or excitement for the future. It's difficult to be up for life when we are down on ourselves. Self-condemnation is the result of not measuring up to our own standards and expectations. We miss the joy of living because we feel we have no right to enjoy ourselves, knowing all we do about our failures and missed opportunities. This becomes a syndrome. Our self-depreciation paves the way for further disappointment.

We need a new heart of love and acceptance, affirmation and encouragement for ourselves. But that will not be possible without a new way of thinking about ourselves. Our hearts need different signals from our brains—a new objectivity based on something ultimately reliable. Only God can do that. We need to exchange our thinking about ourselves for his. "A new heart I will give you!" is an ancient promise from God that we desperately need to hear and receive. To "have a heart" for ourselves is to relate to our inner person with the same love and forgiveness that God has shown us in Christ.

This is the powerful message of John's assurance in 1 John 3:19–24. Apparently the early Christians also suffered from the uneasy frustration of self-condemnation. They had heaped their sins and failures on one side of the scale. The Apostle of Love balances the scales in this liberating paragraph of his letter: "By this we shall know that we are of the truth, and reassure our hearts before him whenever our hearts condemn us, for God is greater than our hearts, and he knows everything."

There's a tonic for our wilted self-image! A thorough exposition of this section is one of the most liberating experiences a Christian can know, John explains the true basis of "having a heart" for ourselves. He shows us how to receive a new heart free of self-condemnation.

It begins by starting a new past. A poster on a wall of an Alcoholics Anonymous meeting room held out a magnificent promise. "Begin a New Past!" We can begin today to live differently in relation to ourselves so that our tomorrows will be part of a new quality of remembered yesterdays.

This is the hope John had in mind when he said, "By this we shall know that we are of the truth." The middle future of the Greek word for know, *ginōskō*, is used. It implies that our future challenges and trials can be part of our new past. We don't have to go on collecting bad memories to be part of the data bank of our hearts. In each crisis or opportunity we can "assure our hearts before him," in his presence, power, and perspective. When we are tempted by self-doubt, we can dare to focus our lives through the powerful magnifying lens of Calvary. God is for us. His resources are available to us. We can open our hearts before him. Assurance is his gift to us. He will be more than equal to what happens in and around us.

This will be the Lord's gift when our "hearts condemn us." We never know when that will happen. Often it occurs when we are awakened in the middle of the night and memories stalk about in our minds. Sometimes it happens in a moment of quiet in a busy day. Reflection turns to remorseful rumination. Other times, it sweeps over us in an unexpected time of pressure. If only we had more wisdom or insight we would have handled things differently. Our self-negating heart tells us: "If you were more adequate, you wouldn't be in this mess. What's wrong with you? The problem has to be your fault!"

We've all known times like that, more than we want to remember—or repeat. John uses the word *kataginōskō*, to know and hold something against someone. It's a feeling of distrust based on past performance. When we feel it toward ourselves, we become immobilized. Note the two words *ginōskō* and *kataginōskō* used in the same sentence. We can

know that we are of the truth or we can know that we can
build a case against ourselves. We are challenged to accept
the former and let go of the latter.

How can we do that? By accepting that "God is greater
than our hearts because he knows everything." He knows
every secret of our hearts, every dream for the future, every
sin and failure of the past. But he knows something more.
Much more! The Lord's omniscience is always linked to his
overarching love and sympathy. He knows what we've been
through, he sees what we've been and done, but he also holds
the picture of what he has intended us to be. All our missed
opportunities are seen in the light of what he's ready to do
with us if we will cooperate with his Spirit. He's never
frustrated by our past. He is the Lord of our future. At this
moment he is offering us the chance to be as forgiving and accepting of that battered person inside us as he is. What a relief!

Now we are ready to consider the gift of an uncondemning
heart. John presses on to that with delight: "Beloved, if our
hearts do not condemn us, we have confidence before God."
This is the converse of the condemning heart. It's not a claim
of perfection but of the consciousness of God's presence. It's
there that we are offered the sure sign of a new heart: confidence.

The word *confidence* in Greek means boldness. It's a great
New Testament term. It was used to describe the intrepid-
ness, forthrightness, and fearlessness of the disciples after
Pentecost. Acts identifies what happened to John himself
after the infilling of the Holy Spirit. The Hebrew leaders in
Jerusalem were astounded by what they observed. "Now
when they saw the *boldness* of Peter and John, and perceived
that they were uneducated, common men, they wondered, and
they recognized that they had been with Jesus" (Acts 4:13).
Quite a compliment!

This helps us to understand what John is trying to communicate in this section of his letter. Boldness is the result of

being with Jesus. Years of experience with the Master, before and after Pentecost, had taught him that fearlessness. Before receiving the resurrected Lord as indwelling Spirit, John's life had been dependent on his own cleverness and talent. He was competitive rather than confident, constantly comparing himself with the other disciples and vying for position. His ambitions were based on his own abilities. The crucification shattered that! But after Pentecost he was filled with power. That gave him boldness to live courageously by the Lord's gifts rather than his own grit. John's capacity to love and care for people, beginning with himself, was the result.

Boldness is the peculiar quality of an uncondemning heart. It expresses the daring of asking God for what we need. John quickly follows his assurance in the presence of God with an explanation of what that boldness before God engenders: "We receive from him whatever we ask."

That's the healing antidote for self-doubt. John could remember well the offer the Lord had made repeatedly. Jesus knew that at times of self-condemnation we would need to have our depleted confidence restored. He knew that God was always more ready to act than we would be to ask. "Now therefore, I tell you, ask in prayer, believe that you will receive it and you will" (Mark 11:24). "And I tell you, ask and it will be given you; seek, and you will find; knock and it will be opened to you" (Luke 11:9). In his own Gospel, John recorded his recollection of the Lords' hope for discouraged disciples. When we are down on ourselves and the results of our efforts, perhaps it's because we have tried to do our thing by our power.

Jesus stretches our vision and reminds us of his post-resurrection availability through the Holy Spirit. "Truly, truly, I say to you, he who believes in me will also do the works that I do, because I go to the Father" (John 14:12). "I say to you, if you ask anything of the Father, he will give it to you in my name" (John 16:23). "If a man loves me, he will keep my word, and my Father will love him, and we will come

to him and make our home with him" (John 14:23). Our
hearts are to be the Lord's home. From within, he guides us to
ask for what he is ready to give.

We can ask for anything in prayer when we meet the qualification John puts forth, "Because we keep his commandment
and do what pleases him." That's the key! Our purpose in life
is to do what will please him. We have only one person to
please. When we are committed to please the Lord, we will
experience a greater pleasure in ourselves than ever before. A
self-condemnatory heart can be healed.

John concludes with a twofold test of pleasing God. We are
to believe in the Name of his Son and love one another. That
implies that we are to accept the power and authority of the
Name for the basic purpose of loving people. Our hearts will
always condemn us if we miss that. Actually, the uneasy feeling is our alarm system telling us we have gotten off track. If
we feel love for others welling up in our hearts, we can be sure
that we have received the result of believing in the name of
Jesus Christ. He will be loving people through us.

The other day a friend of mine said, "I said to myself, 'Self,
listen here!' " In the light of John's stirring message, what do
you have to say to that person inside you? The Lord has used
this passage to help us see and accept that inner self. The
greatness of the One who knows all things helps us to sympa-
thize and forgive. He shows us not only what we've done, but
also what we meant to do and wanted to do. Thomas à Kem-
pis said, "Man sees the deed, but God knows the intention."
The Lord judges us not just by our actions but by the longings
which may not have become actions and the dreams that may
never come true. And yet, that assurance inadvertently becomes the source of strength to dare what we might never
have attempted. Fear of failure is liberated. An old French
proverb says it: "To know all is to forgive all." And God
knows all.

Our hearts have been given a great gift. Love for ourselves.

Knowing that, I can now say with a different emphasis than when I began this chapter, "Have a heart—for yourself!"

PRAYER FOR THE DAY: *Lord, our prayer is that we may allow the Holy Spirit to fill our hearts with the pulsating, surging, exuberant vitality of the gift of love. With boldness we ask that you will teach us to love ourselves as much as you do. We know that when that happens our self-condemnatory hearts will be healed and we can get on with the true business of life—loving others. We really want to have a heart for ourselves today. Thank you for making it so. Amen.*

15.

Testing the Spirits

Beloved, do not believe every spirit, but test the spirits to see whether they are of God.

1 John 4:1

READ: 1 John 4:1–3

I'm no heresy hunter. I find no delight in poking around in people's theology to get the goods of distortion on them. It's when I see what heretical thinking does to confuse people and when I calculate all the time, energy, and money expended on movements rooted in fallacy, that I become alarmed.

My business is people. What happens to them because of what they believe is my passionate concern. I believe we do what we do because of what we believe. When our beliefs are confused, our lives reflect the confusion. It's because I love people that I worry about causes which become eccentric excursions away from the center of truth, or about faddish psychodynamics which replace the Lordship of Christ.

How do we know what's true? How can we discern the best among the many goods offered us today? What is a sure test that any effort is worth our resources? On what basis should we make our choice of a local congregation for worship, fellowship, and study? Which one of the many enterprises seeking to alleviate human suffering is deserving of our contributions? How shall we spend the brief years of our life?

John tells us to test the spirits. My pastor's heart pulses again with the Apostle's. He was concerned about the Christians and the danger of their being pulled in all directions of distorted beliefs and loyalties.

The major problem, as we have seen in an earlier chapter, was that many dear friends had been enticed out of the fellowship by the Gnostic teachers. That left the church with ambivalent feelings. They loved their former members but were disturbed by their newfound beliefs. We all know what that's like; there are people we love whose convictions we find upsetting.

Eventually it's love that draws the line—for their sake, as well as ours, and the purity of the church. John gives us the basis of evaluation. He shows us how to recognize the Spirit whose source is in God, and the spirit that is rooted in the antichrist. The test is the open acknowledgment that Jesus has come in the flesh and is the Christ. Any person who does not confess this basic conviction about Jesus has a source other than God.

We have touched on the Gnostic problem John confronted. Now we must deal with it more completely. The Gnostics had derived their name from the Greek word *gnosis,* meaning knowledge. They boasted a superior and esoteric knowledge about how the world was created, how evil existed, and how an individual could gain a special hidden wisdom about the nature of things. Gnosticism asserted that God was distantly aloof from the world. Creation had occurred as a result of a series of emanations, each more distant from God. The furthest finally created the world. This idea was based on the presupposition that God was spirit and good; the material world was evil and could have no contact with God. He had allowed the creation of the world through separate, delegated emanations, but he had no contact with the world. The idea

that some of these emanations were angelic, and others eventually became antagonistic to God was the source of the explanation of evil in the world.

The simplistic theories were based in philosophic sophistry.
Holding to the idea that all matter was evil, the Gnostics
maintained that flesh was equally evil. But what to do with
the incarnation of God in Jesus Christ? That became the
burning issue in the conflict with the church. The Christians
boldly proclaimed that God had lived in the flesh in Jesus the
Messiah. The Gnostics countered with the teaching that if
Jesus was the son of God, he could not have dwelt in the flesh.
Therefore, they said, he was one of the many angelic emanations from God. He could not have lived as a man, or suffered
on the cross, and did not rise from the dead. As we will note
later, some did accept the uniqueness of Christ, but suggested
that the Spirit descended on the man Jesus at baptism and left
just before the crucifixion.

In addition to the confusion of the philosophic teachers, the
church was also troubled by the compulsions of an ascetic and
mystic brotherhood of Essenes. They had the same shaky intellectual framework as the Gnostics, but were distinguished
by their Mosaic legalism. The strange breed of Essenes har-
assed the church with a demand that the Christians should
fulfill the regulations and requirements of Judaism, becoming
Jews in all respects. They were the vigilantes of their brand of
legalism. Marriage, eating animal flesh, enjoying the body,
and any delight in life's pleasures were open for their judgment. They had elaborate rites and rituals that went way
beyond the Mosaic tradition. The strange blend of Gnosticism, fanatical legalism, and esoteric religious secrets also included worship of the sun and an elaborate gradation of
angels.

All this sounds bizarre until we empathize with what it
must have been like to be a Christian under that kind of pressure. Our religious potpourri is not much better today. We,
too, confront both the equivocations about Christ and the mo-

ralists who believe they can change the world by regulating people's behavior.

John was very direct. We can test the spirits by the Spirit of Christ. He abides in us. Only what deepens our relationship to him is valid. No belief or philosophy which denies that he dwelt in the flesh as the Messiah at the center of history is worthy of any attention. The acid test of any movement or cause is that it lifts up Christ as the only hope, leads people to a relationship with him, and extends the implications of the gospel in the affairs of society. That eliminates a lot of pleas for our donation dollars and for the precious hours of a lifetime.

I have found that John's test works. The desires of people, the need to be accepted, and the voracious appetites of our own egos can lead us down one dead end after another. We need to discern the spirit behind all enterprises and opportunities, as well as that behind religious ideas and organizations. The Christ-Spirit in us will guide us if we are willing. Then we can ask:

1. Is Christ glorified?
2. Do the people involved believe in Christ as Lord and Savior?
3. Is the irreducible maximum of the incarnation at the center: that God was in Christ, reconciling the world; that he lived in the flesh, ministered as the Messiah, died for the sins of the world, was resurrected, and is with us now?
4. Will people be introduced to the gospel in its fullness, and to Christ as personal Lord and Savior?
5. Is the Lord's love the basis of the desire to care for people and their needs?
6. Will it extend the kingdon of God into the lives and structures of society?

The abiding Christ within us will also help us discern the spirit of people. We will be given profound intuitive insight. The Christ in us always answers the Christ in another person.

We know when a person belongs to him. But here again, what he means to them will be exposed by their belief in the incarnation historically, and presently through the Holy Spirit. The test of people's ideas or projects will be the extent to which they are an extension of Christ's love, and to which they will the ultimate good of all involved.

We have been equipped to listen, reflect, feel, and absorb the impact of a person's authenticity or lack of it. Testing the spirits cannot be defined as easy evaluation with no responsibility. If we discern the Spirit of Christ, we are called to be supportive; if not, we are called to caring and concern in order to help the person into a liberating relationship with Christ. We do not need to be "tossed to and fro and carried about with every wind of doctrine, by the cunning of men, by their craftiness in deceitful wiles" (Eph. 4:14). When we know who we are because we know to Whom we belong and who lives in us, we will experience a new discernment and decisiveness.

PRAYER FOR THE DAY: *Lord, life and the people around us present us with a mixed bag of challenges and opportunities. Thank you for showing us that love is not sentimental or stupid. There are lots of good things that may not be your best for us, and even more bad things that may look good, which could scuttle our ship. We trust you, abiding Lord, to give us the gift of testing the spirits. We want to trust you completely and to love people sufficiently so as not to bless what comes from either ego or evil. Show us how, dear Lord, today! Amen.*

16.

The Optimism of an Experienced Pessimist

He who is in you is greater than he who is in the world.

1 John 4:4

READ: 1 John 4:4–6

The other day, a friend gave me a new definition of a pessimist. Jokingly, he said a pessimist is a highly experienced optimist.

I thought about that after the laughter died down. My experience is just the opposite. An optimist is a highly experienced pessimist. True optimism is born out of experiences of Christ's power in the midst of what would make a person pessimistic.

What's it all about, Alfie? Don't ask Alfie, Alice, or Albert. They don't know! But who does? Where can we find the purpose of it all in a world like this? What makes Sammy run? Sammy's the last person to ask!

We look around us. The aspirations we experience in the asphalt jungle leave us no clearly marked path. We try, with Kafka, to "see through the thickness of things." We are tempted to give in to what Camus called "that hopeless encounter

117

between human questioning and the silence of the universe." Like Alex in Anthony Burgess's *A Clockwork Orange,* our eyelids are clamped open, and we are forced to watch the never-ending film of human depravity and ultra-violence until we gag and retch and "creech" for help. We must agree with T. S. Eliot: "Humankind cannot bear very much reality." Finally, we identify with the man who went to his opthalmologist and said, "I'd like to see a little more poorly, please." We cannot live by dread alone!

When we allow ourselves to get in touch with life, we feel the pain, disappointment, and anguish around us. People are irresponsible and society is careless. Evil people enrage us, neutral people upset us, and good people who do little alarm us. The natural world has more than enough catastrophes to balance off its resources and beauty. The institutions of our culture are painfully slow to respond to human need. The church is often anachronistic, communicating more defensiveness than decisiveness. People we love trouble us, and some we depend on to lead us let us down. It's not easy to be optimistic about life or the future.

Unless—! We will be pessimistic until we have a power within us that is greater than the evil in the world.

There was a growing discouragement in the churches to which John wrote. Satan, and not Christ, seemed to be winning the battle with Gnosticism. There was division among the Christians, persecution from civil authorities, and temptations to deny Christ daily. John reminded them of the source of indestructible optimism. They could overcome because "he who is in you is greater than he who is in the world." The indwelling Christ is the only ultimately reliable source of optimism. Trusting him will make an experienced pessimist into an indefatigable optimist with unquenchable hope. Let's take the verse apart and then allow it to flow with all its joy.

Christ himself is the center of our optimism. He faced the evil one and won. Our Lord confronted evil incarnate in people. He did not trust himself to them; he loved them, knowing what they would do. The cross looked like defeat until he vanquished death and rose from the dead. At Pentecost he entered into his people to give them the same power that he had exposed in his life, ministry, and resurrection.

Paul summarized this same assurance for the Christians at Rome. "But you are not in the flesh, you are in the Spirit, if the Spirit of God really dwells in you. Any one who does not have the Spirit of Christ does not belong to him. But if *Christ is in you,* although your bodies are dead because of sin, your spirits are alive because of righteousness. If the Spirit of him who raised Jesus from the dead dwells in you, he who raised Jesus from the dead will give life to your mortal bodies also through his Spirit which dwells in you" (Rom. 8:9–11).

Note that the same emphasis on Christ's indwelling is given by both John and Paul. This was the secret of their optimism in spite of the observable difficulties both faced in living out their faith. They knew that all things were possible through the power of the Person who lived in them. The indwelling Christ controlled and guided their minds, infused their emotions, and fired their wills. The healing strength of Christ engendered physical endurance, and his guidance made them indomitably fearless. Both had been persecuted, imprisoned, rejected, beset with human betrayal and disappointment with fellow believers. Yet, John's word stands: "Christ in me is greater than Satan or his conscripted agents in the world!" And Paul's courageous affirmation rings through the centuries: "For I am sure that neither death, nor life, nor angels, nor principalities, nor things present, nor things to come, nor powers, nor height, nor depth, nor anything else in all creation, will be able to separate us from the love of God in Christ Jesus our Lord" (Rom. 8:38–39).

The Living Bible translation of our text from John helps us to claim the assurance that Christ does dwell in us. "Dear young friends, you belong to God and have already won your fight with those who are against Christ, because there is someone in your hearts who is stronger than any evil teacher in this wicked world" (1 John 4:4, TLB).

This brings out the basic experience which transforms the

pessimist. "You have already won the fight" is an accurate translation of *nenikēkate,* the perfect active indicative of *nikaō,* the calm confidence in the final victory of Christ. It is his victory, not just ours for him. Because he was victorious once and for all on Calvary and Easter morning, we have a continuous victory in what only seems to be a ceaseless battle. The impact of that is that each new problem is an occasion for a fresh realization of his victorious adequacy. We are reminded of John's earlier use of this tense: "And by this we may be sure that we know him, if we keep his commandments." The meaning is: we know that we have come to know and still know him.

There's almost a light touch of a joyous smile in John's assurance that Christ in his readers is greater than the evil one in the world. When we consider what Christ had done and does, we are tempted to laugh at our feverish anxiety over whether he can pull it off one more time in our present problem. We want to shout with relief. "What am I worrying about? Christ won, wins, and will win!" That's the seed from which optimism grows. It's not a simplistic affirmation that things will work out, but that Christ will work out all things for his glory and our good. As one Christ-experienced pessimist to another, I salute the optimist we can dare to be, regardless of what happens. Most of all, I honor the Christ who lives in you.

PRAYER FOR THE DAY: *Lord, you know how discouraged and impatient we become when we think we're in life's battles alone. Thank you for reminding us of the only three things we need to know: your victory is final, it's realizable every day, and it's ultimate for eternity. Our pessimism brought us to you, and you brought us to authentic optimism. In your victorious name. Amen.*

17.

You're Very Special!

Beloved, let us love one another; for love is of God, and he who loves is born of God and knows God.

1 John 4:7

READ: 1 John 4:7–12

The candles on our secluded restaurant table cast a radiant glow on my wife's face. My heart overflowed with love, affection, and gratitude. I felt sheer delight in the person she is.

We were enjoying a lovely vacation alone. There had been time to explore each other's thoughts, feelings, hopes, and hurts. Deeper closeness had grown through leisurely walks on the beach. Prolonged periods of sharing our inner needs had given us both an opportunity to get caught up with the unique person who lives inside each of us.

I reached across the table and took Mary Jane's hand. Our eyes met and expressed the oneness we were feeling. I searched for words which would convey the vibrant joy bursting inside me. A gift, a verbal sacrament, had to be offered somehow to communicate the pleasure that surged within, demanding expression.

"You're very special!" I said.

"Thanks! I feel that. You're special too!" she replied, tenderly.

That exchange of affirmation started a long conversation about what it means to be someone special. To feel special. What contributes to this dynamic inner assurance? We talked about the people who make us feel special. What is it that they do or say that motivates this magic quality of self-appreciation? We agreed that it is way beyond manipulative compliments or solicitous sentimentality. It is the total impact of a person's satisfaction with us in spite of anything we have accomplished and achieved, or failed to do or say.

Making a person feel special means listening to the emerging, evolving person inside, to the potential. It's sensing the never-to-be-repeated miracle of each individual, and the struggle to express that uniqueness. Why are there so few people who make us feel special? What makes it so difficult for most of us to communicate delight and esteem to others—mates, friends, fellow-workers?

Over the years, I have observed that the people who are able to infuse this precious, liberating experience of self-esteem in others are people who feel good about themselves. They feel special and help others to know they are special.

But that's not easy for most people. They are more aware of their shortcomings and inadequacies than their strengths and abilities. The ledger of self-evaluation lists more liabilities than assets. Creative self-love is difficult for many of us, knowing all we do about ourselves. And there's never a shortage of fellow self-negators around to fortify our negative self-image. It's hard to be up for other people when you are down on yourself. It we're not excited about being ourselves, we can be sure no one around us will be excited about himself.

That's rooted in a deeper problem. Many of us were conditioned in childhood to feel that self-appreciation was arrogance. Enjoying ourselves was considered a sure sign of pride. So few people reach maturity being able to say, "I'm glad I'm me!" What we missed was that praise is the one antidote to pride. A deep sense of gratitude for our abilities and talents is the true source of creative self-affirmation. The freedom to love ourselves is the result of the realization that all that we have and are is a gift. The people who make others feel special have this authentic humility. The question is: how can we discover that? John tells us that in this magnificent passage, which is the central theme of his letter.

It's a gift of God. He alone can break the bind of self-depreciation and free us to enjoy being ourselves. It begins with a personal relationship with him, grows with a realization that he is the source of our life, and is expressed in thankfulness for the person he has enabled us to be. The challenge is to accept his attitude toward us as our own attitude toward ourselves. His personal word to each of us is, "I know all about you. The needs and failures. I love you just as you are! You belong to me. I created you. Have cared for you through the years. Blessed you with abilities and talents. Made the future your friend. All is possible. You are very special to me!"

But how can we be so sure? What proof do we have that God knows, cares, and is for us? Something very powerful is needed to contradict and transform our own niggardly attitude toward ourselves.

That's why God came in Jesus Christ. In time, but for all time, he came to reveal his essential nature of giving, forgiving, unchanging love. What he has said about himself and what we're meant to be is ultimately reliable. Jesus was Immanuel, God with us. Through him, he has told us that each of us is favored, that he is pleased with us, and that we are of immeasurable value to him. This is the impact of the Incarnation. God's personal word to us!

The greeting to Mary at the inception of the Incarnation reveals God's attitude toward all mankind. "Hail, favored one! The Lord is with you." He came to erase any doubt that we are his favored people. That favor dwelt bodily in Jesus Christ. The words spoken at the Savior's baptism are now our Father's assurance to each of us. "This is my beloved Son in whom I am well pleased." God is pleased with us! Jesus expressed that in his relationships with people. He inspired confidence and daring. Frightened people became courageous. Failures received forgiveness and a new picture of their potential. The insecure became bold. Self-depreciators were released to celebrate their God-given gifts. And all because of the liberating power of his love for each person.

Now look at the cross and hear God saying, "That's how much I love you!" Christ died for the sin of the world. Sin is not just the bad things we do; it's the debilitated persons we become. The word *sin* means to miss the mark. Three words that delineate its destructive power form an acrostic of the word: it's *S*eparation from God; the *I*ndependence of wanting to run our own lives; and *N*egativism about life, ourselves, and other people God has given us. And yet, God's forgiving love is not dissuaded. Only grace—unmerited favor—can break our resistance to a joyous life.

The cross was a once, never-to-be-repeated, historical revelation of God's grace. John caught the dynamic of that: "In this the love of God was made manifest among us, that God sent his only Son into the world, so that we might live through him. In this is love, not that we loved God but that he loved us and sent his Son to be the expiation for our sins" (1 John 4: 9–10). Before we could earn or deserve it, God loved us. That alone has the power to tip the scales of self-negation.

The resurrection was God's best for the worst that man could do. The victory of Easter morning was the final validation that Jesus was who he said he was, and that his death was the final defeat of the forces of death and darkness. The grave could not hold him. He came back! At Pentecost the same Spirit who had dwelt in Jesus returned in power to indwell a new humanity. The church was born. God the Creator, Savior, and now infusing Spirit made his post-resurrection home in the minds and hearts of his people. A new creation of men and women was unloosed in the world. They became a loved, forgiven, thankful breed of people modeling God's original intention for all mankind. His love for them released them to love themselves and each other. The historical result of God's incarnation was the exclamation, "My, how those Christians love one another!" John wanted that to be said about the churches to which he addressed his letters so long ago.

To discover that today requires a profoundly personal relationship with the Lord. His love must penetrate the depths of our personality. Like a skilled potter, he reshapes the clay of our self-image. A miracle is performed. We are able to surrender our protective, defensive attitudes. They are replaced with the experience of his approval, closeness, and encouragement. What the Lord said of Abraham can be repeated, interposing our own name: "Abraham, my friend" (Isa. 41:8). Dare to say your name—a friend of God! "Abraham believed God, and it was reckoned to him as righteousness and he was called a friend of God" (James 2:23). Or think of Moses. The Lord spoke to him "face to face, as a man speaks to his friend" (Exod. 33:11). And we know so much more of God than Moses did. We have beheld the face of God in Christ. When we love, we have something better than seeing. God abides in us. "Beloved, if God so loved us, we also ought to love one another. No man has ever seen God; if we love one another, God abides in us and his love is perfected in us" (1 John 4:11–12).

This deep relationship with God results in a totally different quality of relationships with people. We are set free to love as we have been loved. That's the key John is talking about. We can open our inner person to others. That frees them to be real with us. Our grace-motivated self-esteem will enable people to appreciate themselves. Greatness is being a person with whom others feel great. Have you ever noticed that some people impress you with how important they are, and others leave you with a feeling of your importance? What a difference. When we are secure in God's love, we will be able to spend our energies on other people, helping them to realize the special miracle of personality they are. William Penn wrote in the preface of George Fox's Journal what people should feel with us: "He was an original and no man's copy." To help people discover God's original, unique strategy for their lives is the exciting purpose of life.

We all need people around us who care enough to know us and share our struggles. We long for a closeness with people who are vulnerable, open friends who believe in us because they believe in themselves. Everyone experiences the aching need to have a few intimate friends who help him grasp the gusto of self-esteem. It's the central calling of parents. The challenge of marriage. The responsibility we all share.

How to begin? That's what we all want to know. I would not want to mock our urgent need for trusted friends and the desire to be a cherished friend to many by easy platitudes. There is a very concrete, specific formula for realizing we are special and communicating to others that they are special.

1. Begin with yourself. Are you delighted by being you? Excited? What stands in the way? Memories? Frustrations? Feelings of inadequacy; self-condemnation?
2. Dare to be intimate with God. Open yourself completely to him. Tell him about present needs and the cellar gang of frightening anxieties in the basement of your mind.
3. Allow the Spirit of God to reveal to you what he's like. Consider his limitless love in Christ, the cross, the defeat of the powers of darkness. Allow him to nourish you with his love.
4. Boldly claim God's picture of you to be the focus of your mind's eye. Dilate to vivid clarity the person he sees you to be. Then picture what you would be if filled with his cherishing favor.
5. Tell God you want to be to others all that he's been to you. Make a list of twelve people who need to know they

are special. Pray for them. Exercise an inspired imagination to picture them as free, life-affirming, self-appreciating people. Thank God it shall be so!

6. When you are with these people, pray for guidance. Feel the warmth of your own "specialness." It will overflow on them. Tell them how much they mean to you. Not just good things they've done; but the great person they are! Focus your attention on them as if they were the only person for your interest and time. Listen to what they say and to what's spoken beneath their words. Touch the raw nerve of their discouragements and feel the pulse beat of their delights.

7. Follow through with a phone call, a letter, repeated contact specifically recalling your concern for the edge of life's adventure on which they are living. Open your heart about your own struggles and victories in daring to be authentic in living life. Tell them about the power available when we dare to attempt those things which we could never pull off without the Holy Spirit. Most people's lives are dull and drab because they are attempting only what they could accomplish in their own strength. You will become a fellow-adventurer with them.

Everyone has the inalienable right as a person to experience self-esteem. That begins with God. But it never ends there. The real test of whether we have accepted the wonder of being an irreplaceable miracle of God is that people feel special when they are with us. Love is not blind. It has the penetrating vision to see through what might have been, to the favored, unique person inside each of us struggling to be free.

PRAYER FOR THE DAY: *Lord, thank you for making each of us special. We are nourished in the depths of our hearts by the realization that we are special to you. Now our concern is for the people in our lives who need to feel special to us so that we can help them to know that they are special to you also. We commit this day to you to be active, contagious communicators of affirming esteem in people. Thanks in advance for your love for each person. Through the limitless love of the cross. Amen.*

18.

Abide and Abound

He who abides in love abides in God, and God abides in him.

1 John 4:16

READ: 1 John 4:13–21

The advertisement for a new kind of digital watch caught my attention. The boldly printed come-on at the top of the ad was arresting. "Finally—a luxury digital timepiece with your own personal message!" The hard sell went on to claim: "Now for the first time, combine an advanced timekeeping system with your own custom message. Attract attention with this six function watch that lights up any message in L.E.D. (Light Emitting Diode) characters. Ideal personalized gift, incentive award, or personal message."

This revolutionary watch promised solid state accuracy, readability, and reliability. The three buttons on the side fascinated me. One could be pressed for a read-out of the time of day, second of the minute, day of the month, and day of the week. Another was for adjusting the time setting. The third button offered the unique feature. A slight touch would light up the letters of personally selected words. You could have up to seventeen letters for whatever message you wanted for yourself or the recipient of the watch. Each time the button was pressed a reminder, affirmation, or slogan would flash in red L.E.D. characters.

You can imagine what that did to my parabolizing mind. It started me thinking about what message I would formulate for a watch that I bought for myself. What would you put on yours? Ideas flowed freely. "God loves you!" "Now is all you have!" "Redeem the time!" "Live to the hilt!" I could have gone on endlessly.

Then I wondered what I would put on the watch for other people. I thought of one for my wife or the children. What about my friends? If I could afford several thousand, what would I want to communicate to the members of my congregation? Soon I was into one of those "if you could say one thing to the people you love, what would you say?" moods. I took a piece of paper and juggled letters to form words that would express my love and concern. Only seventeen characters! Everything from "I love you!" to "You're special" to "Power to you!" competed for my final choice. After a great deal of thought, I selected seventeen characters which, if a person followed the message, would make nothing impossible: "CLAIM WHAT IS YOURS!"

My consistent and urgent hope for the people I love is that they will claim the unlimited riches of God's grace in Jesus Christ. Everything we need has already been offered and made available: love, forgiveness, eternal life, incalculable resources for daily pressures. I could not think of any need I knew about in any of my friends that would not be met if they claimed what is theirs.

Some of you are probably way ahead of me at this point. You guessed it! I next began to wonder what John would put on a digital watch as his personal message for the church. My studies were immersed in the epistles of John when I came across this advertisement. From our meditation on the Apostle's letters thus far, what do you think he would put into a seventeen-characters-or-less message?

"Love one another!" was my immediate choice. But then, after further thought, I was convinced that John might go beneath that admonition to its motivation. He would probably use only six letters. One word and an exclamation point summarizes John's concern for his friends. He could say in one word what it took me seventeen letters to say. His crystalizing watchword would be "Abide!"

John used the word *abide* in various forms twenty-three times in his three epistles. He challenged people to abide in God and to allow God to abide in them. From that magnificent communion everything else flowed naturally. The sum and substance of John's stirring message was "abide and abound."

The word *abide* means to dwell, inhabit, live, lodge, reside, or rest. It implies continuance, faithfulness, and remaining constantly without limit.

That had a dual dynamic for John. We are to abide in God and dwell secure in his sovereignty and love. To abide is to place our total trust in who God is and all that he has done for us. This dependent confidence in his ultimate reliability opens us to receive his Spirit to reside in our minds and hearts.

On the night before Jesus was crucified, his valediction was, "Abide in me and I in you" (John 15:4). Abiding in Christ for us is to become recipients of his death and resurrection. He died to forgive *our* sins and rose to defeat the power of sin and death for us. All that Christ said, did, and does becomes efficacious for us personally as we abide in him. But the power dimension of the Christian life is the indwelling Christ. "He who abides in me, and I in him, he it is that bears much fruit, for apart from me you can do nothing" (John 15:5).

To abide is to abound. We become recipients of plentiful blessings through his constant interventions. We teem with triumph. To abound is to be fully supplied with all that we need to live a daring, adventuresome, exciting, and truly satisfying life.

1 John 4:13–17 builds a crescendo of praise for all the abundance we have been given as a result of abiding. One promise is heaped on another. We are thrilled by all that is ours.

First, we receive the Holy Spirit. "By this we know that we abide in him and he in us, because he has given us of his own Spirit." Enabling power. The Christian life is impossible without the engendering power of the Spirit within us. Everything I need right now for my relationships and responsibilities can be discovered in the gifts of the Holy Spirit: love; wisdom; knowledge; faith; the power to bring healing to broken lives; the capacity to speak truth incisively with grace; the daring to believe nothing's impossible; the endowment of discernment; and the freedom to praise in all eventualities. When the Spirit of Jesus takes up residence in us, his character is reproduced in our personalities. We inadvertently take on the characteristics of love, joy, peace, patience, kindness, goodness, faithfulness, gentleness, and self-control.

Second, abiding frees us to allow God to love us in the deepest dimensions of our inner self. When we confess Jesus Christ as our Savior and Lord, he takes us on as his personal project for reformation and renewal. "So we know and believe the love God has for us. God is love, and he who abides in love abides in God, and God abides in him. In this is love perfected with us." We become empowered to love as we've been loved.

The Greek word for *perfected* has the meaning of having accomplished a purpose. God's love heals our memories of sin and failure. He reconstructs our self-image and enables us to love and accept ourselves. Then he helps us to see people both as they are and as they can become. We are set free to unbind the uptight and bound-up people around us with healing love. The more consistently we abide in his love, the more we are amazed by the flow of love through us. When we are alarmed by our lack of love, it's a danger signal that we need to abide more deeply in God's love for us. Consistent, habitual companionship will make us lovers.

The other day a woman came to me about the tensions between her and her son. We analyzed and plumbed the depths of the distorted relationship. But after we had emptied her emotions of all the hurt and anguish, something—Someone—had to fill her evacuated soul. Her greatest need was to abide, and allow the love-giving Spirit to fill the emptiness. Abiding and abounding gave her ability to love.

Third, abiding casts out fear. Fear is the absence of an assurance of the abiding presence of God's Spirit. It's a sure sign we have drifted away from intimate fellowship with God and a trusted circle of fellow "abiders." We become frightened by people, life's challenges, the unexpected, and the uncertainty of the future, when we are unsure that God is with us and will intervene on time with superlative strength. His promise is, "I will never leave you nor forsake you." I know that to be more sure than the rising and setting of the sun.

Last week I experienced a disappointment which hurt deeply. On the same day I heard the news, I also received an unexpected answer to prayer in another situation that reminded me that God is very much in charge. A closed door was followed by an open door. I need not be afraid when I abide and abound.

John was right. "There is no fear in love, but perfect love casts out fear. For fear has to do with punishment, and he who fears is not perfected in love." The root of fear is an unstable state of grace. Our inner guilt can be healed by God's unmerited favor. When we know we are loved and forgiven, and that nothing that we have done or been can separate us from God, we can face anything and anyone unafraid.

As I write this, I long not to be glib or mock your struggle with fear. We are all haunted with fears at times—fear of failure, the future, the frustrations of our hopes. What has the capacity of making me afraid? How about you? We need to list them out boldly and look at them realistically. But that's only the first step. It must be followed closely with an abiding conversation with the Lord. When we talk to him about each one and ask him to exorcise them with specific healing, we can be set free. Once again the abide-and-abound formula works: as we draw closer in fellowship with the Lord, his love invades the dark places of our fearful hearts with abounding infusion.

Lastly, abiding gives us the motivating power of prevenient grace. "We love, because he first loved us." Prevenience means to go before. One of the most enabling results of abiding in God is that we discover he is always ahead of us in every relationship or situation. There is no person with whom we must deal, no circumstance into which we must go, that he has not been there before us. There is assurance and peace in that. We are not alone. Jesus' words "Lo, I will be with you" articulate a promise that's ultimately dependable. But he is not only out ahead breaking ground. He is the Lord of the future, the creator of possibilities we could never have planned or imagined!

I learned this again in the search for a strategic person for our staff. Months of interviews did not identify the right person. We were tempted to be discouraged. Then, at just the right time, a man I never imagined would take the job was motivated by the Spirit to apply. All during the time we were searching, the Lord was at work preparing the candidate of his choice. The experience prompted me to abide more securely. In my prayers of praise I said, "Lord, you do all things well. Thank you for going ahead to show the way and meeting me in your perfectly prepared answer. Help me to trust you more in the future."

I want to fulfill that supplication. But knowing me, I realize that I may wander from my abiding place in him. Once again he will surprise me by his prevenience.

We are able to love because the Lord not only first loved us but because he constantly loves us. Teeming abundance enables us to abound with joy and confidence. He loves us before we love him. Our love is always a response to his love. He does not love us because we love him. That's self-justifying religion. The Lord is always the initiator. Our "search" for him is because he has already found us. His Spirit has been at work in us long before we took the gospel seriously. It is through his gift of faith that we believe. He motivates every prayer he's ready to answer. Our longing to abide is the echo of his persistent call.

A digital watch with an "abide and abound" L.E.D. readout message may help. But we need not wait for that luxury. The Lord will not allow us to forget. Life's problems and potentials flash the message, and the inner voice of the Lord relentlessly repeats the gracious invitation. I can hear the tender call and recall right now. You do, too, don't you?

PRAYER FOR THE DAY: *Gracious God, thank you for inspiring John so many years ago to write what we are feeling today. In this time of quiet, we want to abide in your presence. Even now we feel our tensions melt away. Our fears are invaded by your love, and our hopes are maximized by your vision of what you are able and ready to do today. Help us to abound in the unsearchable riches of your limitless resources. Go before us to show the way, and help us to anticipate and joyously receive the amazing gifts of love you have prepared for us long before we dared to ask. In the rush and pressure of this day, keep us in the abiding place of power. Amen.*

19.

Raw Courage

This is the victory that overcomes the world, our faith.

1 John 5:4

READ: 1 John 5:1–5

The Duke of Wellington, who defeated Napoleon at Waterloo, recorded in his journal the need for "three o'clock in the morning courage."

We would agree. Before and in the midst of the battles of life, we need courage. Courage is fear that has been on its knees in prayer. Whenever we start thanking God in tight situations, courage begins to flow. It is a quality of spirit which meets danger or opposition with intrepidity, calmness, resoluteness, and determination. Mordecai's words to Queen Esther focus our need for courage. "Could it be that you have been brought to the Kingdom for such a time as this?"

The early Christians to whom John wrote needed to know that they had been born into Christ for a time like that they were facing. The Apostle wanted them to know that their faith could overcome the world. The word *kosmon,* for world, is used here for the composite of all the forces antagonistic to the new life in Christ. Satan was the divisive general of those forces. The company commanders were the leaders of the Gnostic movement which denied the incarnation. The foot soldiers were the antichrist troups who constantly unsettled the Christians' security in Christ. It was not easy to be a Christian in Roman Asia. Ridicule, conflict, denial of employment, harassment, and loss of personal dignity confronted the followers of Christ. Political punishment was always a danger. The church was often forced underground.

John did not offer glib advice. He simply told the Christians they would overcome. "Whatever is born of God overcomes the world; and this is the victory that overcomes the world, our faith." Born of God means begotten of God—called, chosen, given birth as a son or daughter of God. John wanted his people to remember that they were the cherished children of God. As such, they would overcome the world by his power.

The word *overcome* is used here in a verb form that means a continuous victory in the midst of a continuous struggle. *Overcome* in Greek is to achieve victory. That victory would come as the Christians received situational strength for each new attack from the world. The word *victory* is used two further times in the passage to drive home the point. "This is the victory that overcomes the world." Here *victory* and *overcome* are two different forms of the same root, *nikaō:* the victory, *nikē,* which overcomes, *nikēsasa.* The tense that is used now conveys the meaning of a single victory.

An exciting insight is inherent in the study of these words. The victory of Christ over Satan, death, and sin is a single victory in time and for all time. Our acceptance of Christ as Savior and Lord makes his victory our own. We have overcome the world, once and for all, because we believe in Christ and will now live forever. That single victory is the basis of our overcoming courage in the midst of conflict and difficulties. What has been accomplished for us in the past has ever-recurring, fresh application. We are present active indicative overcomers: we keep on conquering with a new victory in each new skirmish with evil. That's the source of our courage.

When we are faced with what seems to be an impossible battle, we need to stop and regather our forces. And what an army we can count on! Christ himself, his victory on the cross, and the memory of previous interventions when he has been more than adequate to help us. The Psalmist gives us a battle song: "Be strong, and let your heart take courage" (Ps. 31:24).

Kagawa once said to a group of frightened friends what we all need to hear. "Brethren, haven't you left something out of your reckoning? Haven't you overlooked the most vital factor of all? You have forgotten God and his limitless power." The legacy of the Lord's legions is in the Master's own hand, written in the red ink of Calvary. "I have said all this to you that in me you may have peace; in the world you have trouble, but courage! I have conquered the world" (John 16:33, Moffatt).

John knew what he was writing about. He had discovered the gift of courage on the resurrection morning. Christ had won. His victory became John's abiding victory on Pentecost when the Lord entered his heart. The long years of conflict—spreading the faith coupled with imprisonment and persecution—convinced him that Christ was able. He had been scared to death often, but the death was of self-interest. Someone stronger than his fears always interceded. The memory of Christ's words to him while he was imprisoned on Patmos still rang in his heart. Look at John's own account: "When I saw him, I fell at his feet as though dead. But he laid his right hand upon me, saying, 'Fear not, I am the first and the last, and the living one; I died, and behold I am alive for evermore. And I have the keys of Death and Hades' " (Rev. 1:17–18).

The symbol of our church's lay training program is of two keys crossed over. We dare to believe that the keys of the kingdom have been given to our people. They can unlock people and set them free from sin and death. I am constantly amazed by the daily courage given to people who are rooted in Christ's victory, and who ask for his power to face reality and the needs of people in the "world" of Southern California. It's no easier to be a Christian in Hollywood than it was in Ephesus or Laodicea. But the same victorious Lord is available!

There are conditions to courage, however. It is the special gift to those who are doing the Lord's work on his strength. Paul could ask, "If God is for us, who can be against us?" The Lord is always for us, but he's not always for what we are doing. Paul said, "I can do all things through Christ who strengthens me." He could do all the things which were guided by the Lord.

Once we are sure of his direction we can be equally sure of the gift of courage. Christian courage is given for carrying the cross of obedience. When what we must do or be is an extension of the cross, we will have the courage Christ had and promised to us. It's as if Jesus were saying to us right now, "The victory which I won can be your victory also. The world did its worst to me, and I emerged victorious. Life may do its worst to you also, and you, too, can emerge victorious. You can possess the courage for the conquest of the cross." Courage is what is given in the face of a difficult and dangerous situation in which we are called to obey the guidance of God. When we feel the clarity of God's direction, we will have the courage of his Spirit.

The reason many contemporary Christians lack courage is that they are not involved in issues or challenges in which the Lord is their only invisible means of support. Most of the things we attempt can be done on our own strength. The adventure of the Christian life begins when we dare to do what we could never pull off without the Holy Spirit. That's when courage is given.

Where do you need courage at this point in your life? Consider what doing God's will in that situation would be. Ask him. When we are involved in following what he tells us to do, the gift of courage will be there at just the right time. We cannot store up courage; it is given in the raging fury of the battle.

John brings us back to the source of an overcoming faith. "Who is it that overcomes the world but he who believes that Jesus is the Son of God?" Not surprising. Belief in Jesus as the Son of God unlocks the power of God for today's struggles. The name of Jesus opens the heart of God for the heat of our battles. Whatever we ask in Jesus' name will be given to us. A good test. Any prayer for courage in the perspective of Jesus' name will be in keeping with his plan and purpose for us. If we are sure of that, courage will be for the "three o'clock in the morning" crises we face at any time of the day or night.

A personal word to close. I have received courage repeatedly in my pilgrimage as a person and leader. When I have been tempted to give up or be discouraged, the Lord has always come with a fresh surge of courage. When I ask for courage and do not receive it, I drop the program or vision like a red hot poker. If the Lord is not in it, I don't want to be. But if he is, and it's part of his will for me, indefatigable courage bursts forth ebulliently from the Holy Spirit.

PRAYER FOR THE DAY: *Lord, you know better than we do what we are facing today. We need your courage. We surrender all our hopes and dreams, prayers, and visions to your perfect will. We want to do what you want us to do. We've learned that that's the only source of your gift of courage. Thank you for the gift today. We know you will be with us. That's all we need to know. In the name of Jesus Christ, who has overcome the world. Amen.*

20.

The Three Witnesses

There are three witnesses, the Spirit, the water, and the blood; and these three agree.

1 John 5:8

READ: 1 John 5:6–10

There's so much for us to learn from both the content and context of this passage. John teaches us how to deal with false teaching, and in so doing gives us a positive test for our own faith. He takes a troublesome situation and uses it to communicate a triumphant truth.

First, consider the context. This particular passage was prompted by the need to counteract a subtle brand of Gnosticism being taught by a philosopher named Cerinthus of Ephesus. John meets him head-on, not with personal exposure or accusations, but with a clear statement of truth.

Cerinthus taught that Jesus of Nazareth became the Son of God at his baptism by John the Baptist in the River Jordan. He asserted that the divine Christ descended on the man Jesus then and blessed his ministry, but departed before the suffering of the crucifixion. Cerinthus and his followers could not abide the thought that God endured the human pain and an-

141

guish of Golgotha. They said it was the man Jesus who was crucified and resurrected. Gnosticism in a refined form! How could pure Spirit endure the shame and suffering of the flesh on Calvary? Their false teaching in response to that question was infecting the Body of Christ, the church.

Note how John deals with his heresy. Now we can understand why he made such a forceful statement about the three witnesses of the Spirit, water, and the blood. The Apostle took the two aspects of the incarnation that Cerinthus affirmed, and added an undeletable third. The blood of the cross could not be omitted. It was absolutely essential for a complete understanding and experience of the love of God revealed in Jesus Christ.

John shows us that the only way to deal with falsehood is to state the truth. The church would be vulnerable to the virus of Cerinthus' teaching only if the basics were neglected. Heresies grow in churches where Christ's life, death, resurrection, and living presence are not preached and taught impellingly. Today we have the Scriptures of the Old and New Testament as the authoritative basis of faith and practice. Healthy congregations are biblically oriented, Christ-centered, grounded in the cross, rooted in the resurrection, and empowered by the victorious Lord. John did not have the Bible as we have it today. But he did have his own personal experience of the incarnation. Everything he taught was based on his firm conviction that "the Word became flesh and dwelt among us." That was the fulcrum of his faith. The basic foundation on which the whole of Christianity turned was that God was in Christ to redeem the world.

John refused to sidestep the mystery of the cross in simplistic, philosophical theories that evaded the depths to which God would go to love and forgive. The words of Jesus himself thundered in John's soul. "I and the Father are one. . . . The Father is in me and I am in the Father" (John 10:30, 38). There was no ambiguity about that! John had heard those words and could never forget that Jesus had made it clear he was the Messiah, the Son of God, the creative power of God. It was after the crucifixion and the Lord's return in the power of the Spirit at Pentecost that this had become an undeniable conviction at the core of John's being. Then he knew that the cross meant more than that a loving friend had died for his followers. The Master whom John had followed was truly Immanuel, God with us.

We can imagine the uncontainable excitement John and the other Apostles felt when they reflected on all that Jesus had said and done. With the help of the Spirit they pieced it all together. John could never forget the first time he saw Jesus and heard John the Baptist shout triumphantly, "Behold the Lamb of God, who takes away the sin of the world!" He didn't appreciate what that meant then, or during the three years that he spent as Jesus' disciple, or even when the Lamb writhed on the cross while John stood watching. It was later, when an empty tomb and an experience of the resurrected Lord became the settled assurance of his life, that John could write, "No one has ever seen God; the only Son, who is in the bosom of the Father, he has made him known" (John 1:18).

And what he made known was sublimely focused in the cross. The Lamb of God had been slain for the sins of the world. God revealed his forgiving heart in the language and symbols of the sacrificial system of ancient Israel. For centuries the sacrifice of the unblemished lamb and the sprinkling of its blood assured the people of atonement. The blood was symbolic of life and sacred to God. But it was never more so than when his own Son became the sacrificial Lamb in a one-time, never-to-be-repeated, ultimate sacrifice for the sins of all people in every age.

That's why the blood of Christ could never be left out of John's preaching and teaching of the atonement. In this passage of his letter, it's as if he were saying, "There are some who are in grave danger because they are trifling with the blood of the cross. Be careful. You cannot leave the witness of the blood out of the incarnation. Your salvation, the forgive-

ness of your sins, and your eternal life are at stake! The divine
Logos, the Spirit who created the universe, dwelt in Jesus and
went to the cross for us. Don't ever forget Whose blood it was
that was shed for you!"

The content of John's teaching is desperately needed in the
church today. We need to be reminded of the stark reality of
what our salvation cost God. It's when all three witnesses become our own experience that we receive the total impact of
the incarnation. The Spirit, the water, and the blood become a
threefold test of the authenticity of our Christian lives. None
can be left out. Christ lived, died, and was raised up that we
might know all three. What happened to Christ now happens
in us. When we reverse the order of the three witnesses it becomes clear to us. The living Christ recapitulates his own life
in us.

The blood opens our hearts. It's the message of the love and
forgiveness of the cross that melts our resistance and independence. At the foot of the cross we know how much God
loves us. Christ suffered for you and me that we might be forgiven and totally reconciled to God. Self-justification is no
longer necessary. We are justified through faith in what God
did for us on Calvary. Alone we can neither earn nor deserve
what is offered. The past is forgiven and each new failure
brings us back to a fresh experience of a love that will not let
us go. God's love knows no limits.

Acceptance of our salvation through the cross leads to our
baptism. It is our experience of death and resurrection.
Whether we are sprinkled or immersed, the basic meaning is
the same. Our old self is surrendered and a new person in
Christ is liberated. We are baptized into Christ and into the
family of God. The symbolic act of baptism is repeated each
time we commit our lives and all our needs to Christ.

Baptism in his Spirit follows naturally. We are filled with
the fullness of the Spirit's power to enable us to live with joy
and assurance. The three witnesses are all gifts of the Spirit.
He creates the realization of our need, brings to our remem-

brance what was done for us on the cross, helps us to respond, and comes to live within us as motivating and driving power. We know what God did in Christ is true, because of our own experience of the incarnation in our own lives. That's what John meant when he said, "He who believes in the Son of God has the testimony in himself. He who does not believe God has made him a liar, because he has not believed in the testimony that God has borne to his Son." To deny what God has said about himself in Christ, and what Christ claimed to be in his loving purpose for us, is to miss the gift offered to us.

We live in a time when the Cerinthian heresy is as rampant as it was when John wrote to the early church. There is a great deal of confusion about Christ in the church and throughout our society. All three witnesses are needed for our witness to our contemporaries. We dare not leave anything out of our witness to what Christ has done for us. Christmas, Good Friday, Easter, and Pentecost are all our reasons for hope in a hopeless age.

Just before I sat down to write this chapter today, I had lunch with a very sophisticated jet pilot. He's been coming to church and has found a new life in Christ. I'll never forget the statement he made at the conclusion of our conversation. It helped me to realize that John's word to the church long ago is fresh for today.

"Thanks for introducing me to the whole gospel. I've dabbled in about every form of philosophy and psychology to find meaning in my life. Now I know that Christ, who died for the sins of the world, also died for me. If you had left out the cross, I would never have found what's been missing in my life. I didn't need Christ as an example only, but I desperately needed a healing and forgiveness of the guilt and frustration within me. Now I feel loved and forgiven. That experience has opened me up to receive the indwelling of Christ himself."

What my friend experienced is what Cerinthus missed. Christ became like us to make us like himself. He took our place so that we might be placed among the beloved of God.

PRAYER FOR THE DAY: *Holy Lord God, we stand in awe today as we realize the total impact of the incarnation. You have gone to the uttermost to love and forgive us. Thank you for the blood of the cross and the assurance that nothing can ever separate us from you because of the once-for-all-time sacrifice of your son. What can we do in response? What can we say? Nothing but this: we love you, Dear Father, because you have first loved us. Through Christ and his cross we humbly pray. Amen.*

21.

Give 'Em Heaven!

And this is the testimony, that God gave us eternal life in his Son. He who has the Son has life; he who has not the Son of God has not life.

1 John 5:11–12

READ: 1 John 5:11–13

The call from the police came one Sunday afternoon. I was told one of my members was in grave difficulty. I rushed to the home. The fire and police departments both had arrived before me. As I rushed up onto the porch, a fireman bashed open a front window. All of the doors and windows had been bolted shut.

The obvious smell of gas gushed out of the broken window. A fireman climbed through and unlatched the front door. We all rushed in and made our way to the kitchen. There we found a young woman with her head in the oven, gasping in the gas, hoping that she could end it all and be free of the tension, frustration, and anxiety of her life.

I'll never forget what she said as I pulled her out and held her. "Am I still alive? I wanted to stop living." After a long conversation about the causes of her despair, I said, "My dear friend, you could end the life of your physical body, but you would spend eternity in the spiritual condition in which you put your head in that oven!"

She was shocked. Her assumption was that ending physical life was final liberation. Not so! Physical death is only a transition in living, not a terminus. There's life after death for everyone. The question is where, how, and with whom we will spend eternity. Death neither ends it all nor ushers us into a state where we can make choices we refused to make in the days of our life. That raises a question.

If you had to make a choice between immortal life and eternal life, which would you choose? If right at this moment you had to make this destiny-determining choice, which would you choose? We all have one of these two already. Some have the other. One conditions what the other will be. We all have immortal life. Eternal life determines what kind of immortality.

Eternal life is a quality with a quantity; immortal life is a quantity without quality. Everyone will live forever. Not everyone will have eternal life.

Our text proclaims the central truth. John gives us the hope and the power to experience it now and forever. "And this is the testimony, that God gave us eternal life, and this life is in his Son. He who has the Son has life; he who has not the Son of God has not life" (1 John 5:11–12).

Immortal life simply means that we will live forever. Eternal life is a quality of life which begins during this life and continues beyond death. It is the new life in Christ which is instigated when we accept Christ as our Savior, allow him to live in us, and grow in a relationship which does not end, but continues to grow in joy and power before and after physical death. The real person inside the housing of our physical body —the composite of mind, emotion and will—is our eternal soul. The purpose of the years of our life here is to establish that communion with Christ which enables abundant life. That life cannot be squeezed into the brief span between our conversion and our death. We come alive here to live the abundant life without reservations, triumphantly and victoriously forever.

Jeremy Taylor said that there is an inseparable relationship between holy living and holy dying. This is John's reassurance to his friends. It's based on five crucial convictions which develop the progression of our understanding of John's testimony about eternal life.

First, God himself is eternal. He has no beginning or end: he is everlasting.

Second, the life of God which is eternal was manifested in flesh in Jesus Christ. He is the creative power of God through whom everything was made. He is Logos; Alpha and Omega; the beginning to the end of all creation. He came not only to reveal God to us but to be God in our midst. More than the truth about God, Jesus Christ is the loving and forgiving heart of God with us. His life was indestructible; the grave could not hold him; death's powers were defeated in his resurrection.

Third, eternal life is mediated as a gift. It is realized in a personal relationship with Christ. When we surrender our total life to him we pass from the power of death over us to the energizing of his life in us. When we are "born again" through a new beginning, death's threat is past. The most crucial death a Christian experiences is the death to himself. That happens long before his physical death.

Fourth, the gift is ours by faith. When we put our faith in Christ and what he has done for us on the cross, our eternal destiny is settled once and for all. By faith we become the container and communicator of the Spirit of God. Our souls are filled and intertwined with his Spirit. The absolute test of our relationship with him is that we know that death cannot separate us from him and that heaven has begun already.

Last, the Lord's life in us is indestructible and indomitable. We are liberated from the root of all fear: the fear of death. We can face life's frustrations and disappointments knowing that nothing can ultimately destroy us.

I am writing this chapter after a long day. I've just come from the Hollywood Presbyterian Medical Center where I visited with a courageous lady named Joy. She doesn't have long to live. Cancer has virulently invaded almost every tissue of her body. The doctors have told her she has only a few days to live. By the time this book is published, she will be more alive than she is tonight. Joy gave her life to Christ years ago. His eternal Spirit lives in her. I'll never forget a trip to the Holy Land with a group from our church. Joy knew she didn't have long to live physically, even then. We had a special time of prayer for her at Capernaum beside the Sea of Galilee. She thanked God for however many more months or years she would live in the housing of her cancerous body. The past couple of years have been a battle with pain and anguish. But through it all she has remained true to her name. Joy!

Tonight she's dying. But death seemed strangely powerless in that hospital room. When I took her hand, she said confidently, "I'm going home soon, you know. But I'm not worried. Christ lives in me. Death will be a comma in the ongoing story of my life. I'm not afraid for I know I'm alive forever."

I left the hospital with the Hallelujah Chorus sounding in my soul. Everything I try to live and preach is validated in this victorious woman. I said to myself, "It's true! People can hear the gospel and respond. Christ can take up residence in their souls. Eternal life is sure in those who belong to Christ!"

As I drove to my study for a few hours of writing before going home, I wondered about the rest of my congregation, my friends around the world. About you! How sure are they? How confident are you? I am reminded that I preach, teach, and write as a dying man to dying men and women. I know how John felt: "I write this to you who believe in the name of the Son of God, that you may know that you have eternal life."

I have a wonderful friend who reminds me often of my purpose. He often prays with me just before I go into the sanctuary to lead worship. Before he leaves, he always gives me a parting shot. "Give 'em heaven!" Not a bad challenge for a preacher—or for any of us. We have been given the power to share Christ's love with people and to help them know him. We can give them the gift of heaven.

I had a dream about that one night. I pictured the people in my congregation standing in an open field. Then the earth began to quake and a gaping fault began to widen. I saw people I love with one foot on each side of the separating earth. With frantic desperation they tried to straddle the yawning opening. Then I saw the Lord on one side beckoning the people to leap on his side. "Jump!" I cried, "Leap on the Lord's side!" A choice had to be made. The dream was a sublimation of my daily concern: that the people I love so much would find Life in the midst of their living.

The church of Christ has aptly been called "the company of the resurrection." Not just the place where eternal life is preached, but the joyous fellowship of those who are alive forever. Every Sunday is to be a celebration of the resurrection so that every day can be an experience of deathless life.

Paul put it in undeniably piercing words in Romans 6:23: "The wages of sin is death." Sin is separation from God, rebellious self-determination, imperious independence which makes us impervious to the Lord's love and purpose. The end of that is a death that sets a demarcation: without a vital relationship with him we will spend eternity separated from God and all of the beauty and blessings we vicariously enjoy now.

But now look at the second half of Paul's sentence. "But the free gift of God is eternal life in Christ Jesus our Lord." Our sin of separation is forgiven and we are given the gift of not only living forever but eternally in close, intimate joyous union. The shortness of time and the length of eternity shock us. We are ready to listen to Paul's simple steps given later in Romans: "If you confess with your lips that Jesus is Lord and believe in your heart that God raised him from the dead, you will be saved. For man believes with his heart and so is justified, and he confesses with his lips and so is saved" (Rom. 10: 9–10).

The key which unlocks heaven, now and forever, is belief in the inner heart and unashamed confession in word. We can be sure that we are alive in a quality of life which death cannot end. Then we can be absolutely sure about the future. "But if Christ is in you, although your bodies are dead because of sin, your spirits are alive because of righteousness [rightness with God]. If the Spirit of him who raised Jesus Christ from the dead dwells in you, he who raised Jesus Christ from the dead will give life to your mortal bodies also through his Spirit which dwells in you" (Rom. 8:10–11).

A young man sat across from my desk. He said, "Why all this talk about eternal life? I want one life at a time. Let me live this one now. I'll worry about the other one later." My response was, "But think of all that you're going to miss between now and then." I tried to tell him about the reality of eternal life now. How I wish I could tell you a success story that ended with the brilliant, handsome athlete accepting Christ. This story doesn't end that way. The young man died in a tragic auto crash two weeks later. He had refused the gift of life eternal, thinking he had all the time in the world. Now he has all the time of infinity without the joy he refused during his twenty-two years. He has immortality without eternal life.

After Paul had soared with sublime rhetoric in explaining the new creation and the affirmation that we can be new creatures in Christ, he said, "Behold, now is the acceptable time; behold, now is the day of salvation" (2 Cor. 6:2).

Christ's great declaration of his gift to us ends with a question. "I am the resurrection and the life; he who believes in me, though he die, yet shall live, and whoever lives and believes in me shall never die. Do you believe this?" (John 11: 25–26). How we answer determines whether or not eternal life will pervade our immortality.

PRAYER FOR THE DAY: *Eternal God: I want to be sure right now that I am not only alive forever, but have come to know and love you so that I can spend eternity in the full realization of the joy of life with you. Amen.*

22.

P.P.T.A.--How to Pray with Confidence

And this is the confidence which we have in him, that if we ask anything according to his will he hears us.

1 John 5:14

READ: 1 John 5:14–15

Recently, I announced a seminar on prayer with the title, "P.P.T.A.—The Secret of Prayer." Many people came because they wanted to know the secret. Some others said they were intrigued by what the letters P.P.T.A. meant. The letters stand for words that have unlocked for me how to pray with confidence. I have discovered an insight that has changed my life and revolutionized my praying: prayer power through awareness.

A few years ago, I began to wonder why my prayers were not effective. I took time each day for a quiet time for prayer, but received few answers. In each opportunity or difficulty I prayed with vigor, but did not receive the power I longed for and desperately needed. I consumed every book on prayer I could find, hoping to find the solution and have the hunger within satisfied. My study of the dynamic Christians of the ages revealed that they were empowered by prayer, yet my

154

prayers seemed like a monologue rather that a dialogue. The only voice I heard in response to my prayers was the echo of my own imploring voice.

Then one day, my reading through the New Testament brought me to 1 John 5:14 and 15. I had read the passage many times before, but had never seen the secret I discovered that day. In fact, my ordination examination in Greek, years before, had included this passage, and my exposition at that time did not give me the insight I found on the day the Holy Spirit taught me to pray on the basis of this text. The revelation made all the difference for me.

John's words written to help the early Christians flashed with wisdom as if they had been written just for me. Verse 15 opened the treasure of verse 14. John wanted his friends to pray with confidence. Remember from previous chapters that confidence is translated from the Greek word for boldness. I needed boldness in my prayers; I had gotten to the place where I almost apologized for daring to ask anything from God, always fearing that I might ask for the wrong or selfish thing. John got through to me: if we asked anything according to God's will, he would hear us. I had not been asking according to the Lord's will. But how could I be sure of his will? Have you ever shared that problem? Then verse 15 was illumined by the Spirit: "And if we know that he hears us in whatever we ask, we know that we have obtained the requests made of him." The Greek word for "ask," "requests," and "made" in this verse all come from a common root, *aiteō*. "Ask" is *aitōmetha;* "requests" is *aitēmata*; and "made" (or "asked") is *eitēkamen*, the perfect active indicative of *aiteō*, to ask while abiding in calm confidence.

The message of these verses forced me to reverse my prayer time percentages. Up to that time I had spent 90 percent of my prayers telling God what I needed, and 10 percent listening to him. My listening time usually followed, rather than preceded, my intercessions and supplications. When we ask according to God's will, we know that we have already obtained the request. We are to ask while we are abiding. If we abide in our prayers, what we ask for will more closely approximate what the Lord wills for us. That means we should abide until we are aware of what the Lord is ready to give. Then we can pray with boldness, knowing he is ready to answer according to the enlightened understanding of his will. Confident prayer became 90 percent listening for awareness, and 10 percent articulating my requests. Thus prayer power comes through awareness of what the Lord wants us to pray for.

A very personal illustration of this is in the experience a couple had praying for me as their pastor and friend. They felt the urge to pray for me. They had both positive and uneasy feelings about what my needs might be. Out of love they asked me what I needed them to pray for in intercession. I tried to tell them as honestly as I could. And yet, as I related my analysis of my need, I was aware that there were very personal, inner needs I was not including. The next day they went to prayer with the data they had from their own gracious observation and from my guarded analysis. For some reason, that day they felt led to be quiet for a long period of meditation before they asked God for anything for me.

The hour set aside was almost entirely used for listening specifically about me. A humbling, gratifying realization that they cared that much! While they were quiet, the Lord broke through, prompting an urge in them to pray about the very thing I had guarded from them. How foolish my reserve had been! They then prayed specifically for the challenge I was facing which the Lord had revealed to them. When they told me about it later, they were very gentle. "Lloyd, we meditated on what we thought you needed and what you said, but this is what we were guided to pray for you." These two prayer warriors related the exact thing I needed most. That was the last time I have ever guarded my true need from those two or from hosts of others who support my ministry in prayer.

Subsequently I have spent long periods in silence, practicing what I call awareness meditation. We all have a strange mixture of presuppositions, preconceptions, and prejudices about what we think people need or situations require. We carry on a long monologue in prayer, informing God of what he ought to do. How patient he is! There is so much we don't know or understand. He sees with penetrating x-ray vision into the minds and hearts of people for whom we would pray. Each challenge we face is part of the tapestry of his plan. How dare we tell God what to do?

A friend of mine analyzed a conversation with a mutual friend who was facing a grave problem. "What did you advise?" I queried. "He never asked for my opinion. We spent hours together. He talked on and on. When I was about to share my insight, he ended the conversation." How like our prayers with God.

Carl Sandburg said that we need to rediscover ourselves in creative solitude. Not only ourselves, but God—and his perspective on our complexities. Thomas Edison said he listened from within. That's fine if the voice within is God's. I like Oliver Wendell Holmes's insight: the trouble with our minds is that they are like checking accounts, and the reason we are overdrawn is that we haven't put anything in. Often we pay without letting God make a deposit of data which may never have occurred to us.

Prayer is not a device to get God to do our will, but a means by which our petitions may be redirected according to the will of God. One of the most demanding things Jesus said about prayer was that it requires time to know the will of God. "Therefore, I tell you, whatever you ask in prayer, believe that you will receive it, and you will" (Mark 11:24). With a power like that available, we need to be sure of what we ask.

During this past year our church has sponsored a Saturday each month called a "Day of Discovery." In addition to Bible study about intimate prayer, we have set aside long periods for silent meditation. We helped each person focus the hurts and hopes he or she wanted to take into the time of creative listening. The people's evaluation of the day indicates that those hours of silence gave them insights and discernment which had not occurred to them before they were quiet. Many of the people found it difficult to center on God and block out the noise of their overinvolved and busy lives. Some found that only after a long period of concentration on God and his love could they open themselves to hear what he was trying to say to them. What alarms me is that, in most cases, people were given wisdom which has subsequently unravelled the personal, interpersonal, and social needs they had finally been enabled to pray about creatively. The question I keep asking myself is: What if they had not learned to meditate until they had a breakthrough to awareness?

I should not be alarmed. Think of how long I was a Christian before I learned this simple 90-10 formula division of listening and speaking. I am very aware that most of us miss the power of prayer and many of the blessings God is ready to give, simply because we will not take the time for God to tell us what he is more ready to unleash than we are to ask. It's part of the mystery that God waits to bless us until we ask for what blessings we really need.

The other evening at our church officers' Session meeting, we used these verses from 1 John as the basis of our Bible study and prayer in the koinonia time which precedes our business meetings. No church in America has greater opportunities or challenges than ours. (If you don't feel that way about your church too, something's wrong.) All of the officers and staff have hopes and dreams for our church that could take a hundred years to realize. That's as it should be. Some are wish-dreams; some are projections of memories of what worked before; some are nonbiblical and culturally induced. Most every church leader in any local congregation has a mixture of all three for his image of what the church should do and be.

At this particular meeting we tried to focus on loving concern for the future of our church. Then we took time to be quiet. When we shared the results of our awareness meditation, we were all surprised by the difference between our ideas and the Lord's revealed will. When we take time to be quiet, we are astounded by the adventuresome things God has in mind; also by the fact that a unity of vision is given. We never allow a proposal to come on the floor of a Session meeting until it has been previously distributed for prayer and meditation. We dare not swagger out ahead of the Lord. Prayer power is given to leaders who will wait on the Lord. Zephaniah has quoted the Lord's cardinal condition for leadership: " 'Therefore wait for me,' says the Lord" (Zeph. 3:8).

A verse in Isaiah has helped me to know that the answers to some prayers are delayed until our petitions are developed. There's no such thing as an unanswered prayer, but there are lots of prayers which seem unanswered because we have not asked God how to pray. Isaiah knew the reality of that. "Therefore the Lord waits to be gracious to you; therefore he exalts himself to show mercy to you" (30:18). When I think of the many times God has not given me what I thought I needed, I am very thankful. If I had received some of my requests, it would not have been good for me or the people I love. In the waiting period the petition was perfected. After I was given the gift of discernment to know what to pray for, the answer came speedily.

All of this leaves us with a wonderful sense of being loved. How good of God to be willing to reveal his strategy to us so that we could pray cooperatively with him. The greatest gift of prayer is communion with God himself. Perhaps the reason he withholds a quick response until we ask for his will in knowing what to ask, is that he wants us to abide in a loving companionship.

Jesus concluded his parable on the importune neighbor who needed bread with the secret. "If you then, who are evil, know how to give good gifts to your children, how much more will the heavenly Father give the Holy Spirit to those who ask him?" (Luke 11:13). The most magnificent gift God can give is his own Spirit. He waits for us to ask. Whatever else we receive as instruction about how to pray, if we have the sublime companionship and superlative power of the Holy Spirit, anything else is secondary.

Some specific steps may help, in summary.

1. Set aside definite periods for meditation every day.
2. Spread out the needs and concerns on your mind.
3. Allow God to guide your thoughts through creative awareness.
4. Write down what the quiet time revealed.
5. Pray with boldness, thanking God in advance that what he has guided you to pray shall be so on timing and according to his perfect plan.

PRAYER FOR THE DAY: *Lord, I want to put into practice the amazing thing John has given me in these two powerful verses. Right now, I commit myself to prayer power through awareness. I want to take time now, and each day, to listen before I talk, so that what I pray I can pray with boldness. Thank you for the gift of communion with you in prayer. Through the name which unlocks the power of your heart, even Jesus Christ. Amen.*

23.

Intercessory Prayer

> *If any one sees his brother committing what is not a mortal sin, he will ask, and God will give him life for those whose sin is not mortal. There is sin which is mortal; I do not say that one is to pray for that. All wrongdoing is sin, but there is sin which is not mortal.*

> 1 John 5:16–17

READ: 1 John 5:16–18

William Law said, "There is nothing that makes us love a man so much as praying for him."

Intercessory prayer is a gift. We become partners with God in the accomplishment of his purposes in the people around us. Prayer for others enables us to share the heart of God. The more we pray for people, the more we will be able to love them as God does. To intercede means to pass between, to go to God on behalf of another. We have been entrusted with the power to change the lives of people around us through prayer.

Quote: intercessory prayer

John continues his thoughts on prayer by focusing our attention on intercessory prayer for people who are in trouble because of their failures and rebellion against God. How do we pray for people who are ruining their lives and those of the people around them through compulsive and habitual sin? The Apostle wages into a subject we need to think about. We all have friends and acquaintances for whom our hearts ache.

Some disturb and distress us; others anger and enrage us. What shall we intercede for in their lives?

The Apostle tells us that there are two kinds of sins: those that are not mortal and those that are mortal. We need to be sure we understand the difference.

The forgiveness of God is freely offered for all sin. When we see a person who has failed or missed God's best for him, we are to pray that God will bring him to the point of confessing his sin, so that he can thus receive forgiveness. The force of John's admonition to pray for people in trouble is that God will honor our prayer and actually intervene to rescue them from actions, attitudes, and patterns which are debilitating their lives. Prayer is our potent alternative to criticism, judgmentalism, and negativism. People do what they do because of what they are inside. Only God's love and our acceptance can help them face the distorted motivations for what they do. Prayer releases the power of God for those inner needs, and it changes our attitudes toward the people themselves.

Whenever we learn of a sin in another person's life, it's a signal to pray. God has entrusted us with the knowledge so that we can cooperate with him in helping the person to overcome not only the sin but the needs which prompted it. He will give us insight and wisdom. It may be that he will use us in a loving confrontation or an offer to help. But be sure of this: talk to God about a person's sin before you talk to the person! We need his sensitivity and compassion—and timing. He will prepare a person for what he's prepared us to say. Often he will boil the sin to the surface so that the person confides in us about the very need in him or her that has troubled us. Then our task is to help the person confess the sin to God. Be careful not to give cheap grace. The forgiveness of God is available through Christ and the cross. But it cannot be appropriated until sin is acknowledged and confessed.

This gives us the key to unlock what John means by the sin which is mortal. The Greek is *pros thanaton,* meaning the sin which is leading toward death. The implication is that there is a sin which ends in death; that is, one which robs a person of eternal life. We are left to ponder what John meant. What sin will deny a person life with God now and forever? Is there an unforgivable sin?

Jesus identified the unforgivable sin as sin against the Holy Spirit. He said, "Whoever blasphemes against the Holy Spirit never has forgiveness, but is guilty of an eternal sin" (Mark 3: 29). At first that seems to contradict the grace of God. Not so. Jesus acknowledged the awesome power of free will. The scribes and Pharisees had said he had an unclean spirit. They declared that he was possessed by the prince of demons, Beelzebub, and refused to believe that the Spirit of God in him was the power behind his words, acts, signs, and wonders.

Resistance to the Holy Spirit is the unforgivable sin. The ministry of the Spirit is to enable us to accept Jesus Christ as Savior and Lord. The impulse and impact of the Spirit is to bring us to the end of ourselves, and to the confession of our need for forgiveness and reconciliation. God never refuses to forgive, but we can refuse to ask. Fulton J. Sheen put it sharply: "The really unforgivable sin is the denial of sin, because, by its very nature, there is now nothing to be forgiven."

The mortal sin John referred to was like that. There were those who refused to believe in Jesus Christ as the Son of God and Messiah. Much worse, there were those who had believed but had fallen under the influence of the antichrist. Eternal life was available only through Jesus Christ. To deny him was to seal one's destiny. John is not talking about a chance denial through weakness or pressure, but a compulsive, persistent apostasy. It is more than resisting Christ's lordship over an area of our lives; it's a total denial of our relationship with him. That sin is unforgivable as long as it's not confessed.

How shall we intercede for people we know and love who consistently and compulsively refuse to acknowledge Christ as Lord of their lives? John's answer seems very harsh and negative at first reading: "There is sin which is mortal; I do not say that one is to pray for that. All wrongdoing is sin, but there is sin which is not mortal." In the context of the total sweep of John's thought in his letter, I think the sense of that statement is that there's a point when resistance to Christ is not *yet* mortal. There is a time before resistance is hardened into renunciation. Since we do not know when that happens in another person, our challenge is to continue to pray without ceasing. God never gives up, even when people give him up. We can only respond with awe that he loves us so much that he will not deny our freedom of choice. We can say "no" so long that we can't say "yes." Before that occurs in a person's life, our task is to pray that he or she will respond to God's love impinging on his or her mind and heart.

My experience is that God answers that prayer when we are most tempted to give up hope for a person. There have been times when I was completely discouraged and hopeless about a person that the miraculous turning point occurred. Knowledge of those occasions has alarmed me never to resist the Holy Spirit's impulse to pray for someone who is resisting him.

Our calling as intercessors is to ask the Lord to guide us in the construction of our prayer list. He will put people on our hearts he wants to bless through our prayers. Up to this point in my prayer life, God has never told me to stop praying for people because he's finished with them!

PRAYER FOR THE DAY: *Dear God, you have called us to the awesome opportunity of intercessory prayer. Today, we want to pray for people you have put on our prayer agenda who are in trouble because of sin in their lives. We know from our own lives the pain and anguish our own sins have caused us and other people. Out of gratitude and praise for your forgiveness of us we want to pray for people we love. Lord, before it's too late, open their hearts to your love. Now in this time of intimate conversation with you, show us how we can be part of your pursuit of them. Enable us to know what to be and say, when and how we are to incarnate your love by intervening with comfort or confrontation. In the name of Christ, your love that knows no limits. Amen.*

24.

Diminutive Gods

Keep yourselves from idols.

1 John 5:21

Read: 1 John 5:19–21

Who or what competes with God for the loyalty of your heart? John challenges us to consider that in the concluding words of his first letter. "My little children, keep yourselves from idols." I like the Living Bible translation of that verse: "Dear children, keep away from anything that might take God's place in your hearts." Westcott puts it, "Keep yourselves from all objects of false devotion."

John wrote his letter in Ephesus, a city filled with idolatry, and the pollutions of the temple of Diana surely were on his mind. Immorality was limitlessly condoned. Criminals could find safe asylum in the presence of the temple. Charms were sold which were supposed to bring magic powers over a person's destiny. Icons of the temple had produced a lucrative business for the silversmiths. People bought the icons in belief that the power of Diana would be resident wherever the icons were carried.

Ephesus was also a city of magic and sorcery. Every form of cult and the occult was rampant there. Astrology flourished. Incantations, exorcisms, and mystical religion were available on most every street corner.

The city was also famous for its games and the adulation of the physical body. This blended well with the sensuality and distorted sexual practices of the city.

Added to all that was the cult of Caesar worship which pervaded the then-known world. Christians in Ephesus, and throughout Asia, were often faced with a trial of their ultimate loyalty by being required to make a choice between Christ and Caesar. Domitian demanded Caesar-worship in Ephesus until his death in A.D. 96, ordering people to show their loyalty by burning incense before Caesar's bust.

No wonder John concludes his letter the way he does! It was no simple matter to be a Christian in Ephesus, or any of the cities to which this letter was sent. The diminutive gods of false religion, sensuality, black magic, political safety, and economic security were tempting idols. It was a grisly, gutsy world in which to dare to say, "Jesus Christ is my Lord!"

The same idols are still beguiling us. Money, security, pleasure, people, careers, and possessions are still idols which demand us to worship them rather than God. Our idols can be anything or anyone which threatens to occupy the throne of our hearts. God-substitutes can be very demanding of our time, money, and energy.

Our problem is juggling our idols while at the same time offering our commitment to Christ. In fact, our syncretism is so subtle that we use Christ to keep our idols. We set our priorities for our personal goals, our image, our families, and our future plans; then we not only ask Christ to bless them, but help us achieve them. We keep Christ in the idol-polishing and maintenance business!

There's a deeper cause. It's possible to believe in Christ and still have self on the throne. Self is still the most dangerous diminutive god. We say we are Christians, attend church, pray our prayers, and become involved in social causes, all while our lives remain in our control. We would be the first to admit our need for Christ—but to accomplish our predetermined plans and purposes. Christ is in our lives and often on our minds, but does not reign in our hearts. Prayer becomes our effort to get the Lord to march to the demanding drummer of our self-will. We do not report in for his marching orders, but call in the reserves of his strength for *our* battles. We are still commander-in-chief!

In this pattern we can accommodate the most forceful preaching and teaching about idols. We nod approvingly when a preacher takes on the diminutive gods. Preach it, parson! We affirm the exposure of the popular icons of the world. We wag our heads in consternation and look around in satisfaction, enjoying the fact that the gospel is being preached so relevantly for other people. Our citadel of self-control is still intact. The carnality of our lives has not been touched.

But then our eyes drift back over the verses which preceded John's jolting words about idols. We can readily agree with verse 19: "We know that we are of God, and the whole world is in the power of the evil one." Hear, hear, John! We could end the matter there, but John the Apostle doesn't. He goes on and puts us eye to eye, heart to heart, with Christ himself. We become less chipper with our cheap salvation. "And we know that the Son of God has come and has given us understanding, to know him who is true; and we are in him who is true, in his Son Jesus Christ. This is the true God and eternal life." What does he have to say about our utilitarian opportunism?

Jesus' parable of the wicked vinedressers helps me to understand my most dangerous idol. Remember the story? The owner of the vineyard rented out the vineyard, with its abundant vines, its many wine presses and vats, a protective wall, and a tower. All the vinedressers had to do was enjoy the vineyard and its profits, and at the end of five years pay a third of the produce to the owner. That was the rub. The self-possessed and determined vinedressers began to believe and act as if the vineyard were theirs. They had worked it, fertilized, and pruned the vines, and arduously harvested the crops. "The vineyard is ours! What right does the owner have to claim any of the produce? It was our sweat and labor that developed the vineyard." When the delegation of servants came to collect, they stoned and cast them out of the vineyard. When the owner's son came, they killed him, hoping to possess the inheritance forever.

This parable of self-exposure of the heart of God was told by Jesus during his last week in Jerusalem before he was crucified. It helps us to come to terms with what he believed to be his mission in Israel, the vineyard of God, and in our hearts. The transition from his, to ours, to mine, is never immediate but grows over a long time. We may even invite the Lord into the vineyard and share the tithe of our efforts, but he is still little more than an honored guest in the vineyard. We are convinced it belongs to us!

But that's the one thing the Lord will not be. He will not take his place on our shelf of beautifully displayed idols. He is Lord of all or not at all.

That makes me want to say, then pray, and finally sing with abandoned commitment the words of Andrew Reed's hymn:

> "Holy Spirit, all divine,
>   Dwell within this heart of mine.
> Cast down every idol throne;
>   reign supreme, and reign alone."

PRAYER FOR THE DAY: *Holy, holy, holy, Lord God almighty! Heaven and earth are filled with your glory. Praise and honor be to you, Lord most high. Ruler of the universe, reign in us. Lord of all creation, re-create our hearts to love you above all. Blessed Christ, abide in us and conquer all lesser loyalties. Banish the idols. We surrender the idol of self. Transform our passions until they burn white-hot with commitment to you alone. Then we will abide in you as our only reason for life, now and forever. In your powerful, idol-diminishing name. Amen.*

25.

Love in Truth

Whom I love in the truth, and not only I but also all who know the truth which abides in us and will be with us forever.

2 John 1–2

READ: 2 John 1–6

The invitation for a gathering of church leaders in the community caught my attention. "There will be an informal gathering of community religious leaders for a time of fellowship. We need to set aside our doctrines and perception of truth, and just be together as friends. There will be no speakers or long agenda, just pure fellowship!"

I must admit that the possibility of a meeting without speeches or agenda was attractive, but I wondered what the meeting would accomplish. The words *pure fellowship* intrigued me. What was intended was a time of pleasant visiting over a cup of tea. I am always amused, and sometimes alarmed, by the use of the word *fellowship* in church circles. We think of it as camaraderie and conviviality, something we can produce. The New Testament does not use the word that lightly. It means to have in common. But what we hold in

common determines whether we will receive the gift of fellowship or not. It is an awesome gift given to those who have
Jesus Christ as the basis of their relationship. It doesn't happen just because we are together.

Let's face it: there are different levels of relationship. We
all have friends, associates, neighbors, and loved ones with
whom we cannot have fellowship. We can share mutual goals
and concerns, even romantic involvement, and not be in fellowship. Only Christ can produce that—and only if both persons or a group of people share an ultimate commitment to
him as Savior and Lord of their lives. Our perception of truth
about him cannot be set aside in order to have fellowship.
There is an irreducible truth about him that enables fellowship in the deepest biblical meaning of the word.

There is a growing concern in the American church about
the lack of fellowship in local congregations. Perhaps the reason is that we have thought of it as the least common de-
nominator for believers instead of the highest expression of
love rooted in a continuing experience of the truth.

That was John's concern when he wrote a second letter, this
one to "the elect lady and her children." What a beautiful
designation of the chosen, called-out people of God. It means
a particular church, most likely in Roman Asia, and its members. 2 John is brief—the length of a papyrus sheet, about
eight by ten inches. And yet on that one sheet has been pre-
served a vital, undeniable message about Christian fellowship.
The letter could be summarized in one word: truth. John
wanted the Christians in this church to know that there could
be no lasting fellowship with God, or between Christians,
without a basic assumption of truth about Christ. Love and
truth are Siamese twins for the Apostle. The life of the one is
dependent on the other.

The circumstances motivating this letter are not unlike our
own today. The church to which it was written was struggling
to maintain the fellowship of its members in the face of varie-

ties of belief about and experiences of Christ. The Gnostic heresy had stretched the fabric of the fellowship.

A recapitulation of what we learned earlier is helpful. There were those who denied the essential truth of the incarnation. They questioned whether Christ had actually lived in the flesh as the Word of God. Others suggested that the Spirit had come upon Jesus at the baptism and left before the Crucifixion. Some others asserted that Jesus was one of many emanations from God, little more than a phantom manifestation. Still others resisted the moral implications of the Lordship of Christ. John wrote to call the church back to the truth. The future fellowship of the church depended on it.

John gets right to the point in the opening of the letter. He affirms the quality of his own relationship with them. "Whom I love in the truth" is more than an accolade; it is the theme of what he wants to say to the struggling Christians about their church. The key phrase explains not only how he feels about them, but what he longs to have be the unifying basis of the church's life. He wants them to love one another in truth. Our task is to discern what that means for us.

For John, truth was a synonym for basic Christian doctrine. The word embodied the composite of all that Christ was, did, and is. More than that, Christ himself is the truth—about God and the real nature of things. Jesus said, "I am the way, the truth, and the life." If we define truth as essential reality, Christ as truth reveals the way to God and the way we were intended to live.

Truth about Christ can never be separated from the incarnation. Immanuel, God with us, was born, lived among us, died for our sins, was resurrected from the dead, and is with us as reigning Lord of all life. As the present Lord, he loves us and loves others through us. To love in truth is to be a channel of his love. Mutual love in Christ is possible only between those who acknowledge him as Savior and Lord. Belief in the incarnation enables his incarnation in us. From within, he motivates the authentic, giving and forgiving, unlimited and unrestrained love we can have for each other in the fellowship. Having differences about Christ debilitates our capacity to love in his name and by his power.

Jesus stressed truth throughout his ministry. He believed he was God's truth in the world. The words he spoke were the Creator's truth about what life was meant to be. He stated it clearly: "I proceeded and came forth from God; I came not of my own accord, but he sent me" (John 8:42). That's why he called people to take what he said seriously. "If you continue in my word, you are truly my disciples, and you will know the truth, and the truth will make you free" (John 8:31–32).

The deeper our experience of the truth, the more free we are to love. We not only know the truth about God and his love for us, but we can dare to accept the truth about ourselves. The more we acknowledge our need, the greater is our experience of God's grace. Absolute honesty about our character and personality not only opens us up to receive forgiveness and remedial remolding, but it also opens us up to be truthful, real people with others. True fellowship grows in that context.

The prayer Jesus prayed on the night before he was crucified reveals the purpose of his incarnation and his longing that his people would experience oneness with one another. The prayer is an awesome look into the very heart of God. It gives us the intention of the incarnation and the conditions of true communion as fellow believers.

Note first why Jesus came. "Father, the hour has come; glorify thy Son that the Son may glorify thee, since thou hast given him power over all flesh, to give eternal life to all whom thou hast given him. And this is eternal life, that they may know thee the only true God, and Jesus Christ whom thou hast sent" (John 17:1–3).

Now sense the Lord's concern for his disciples and the central truth which he knew would bind them together. "I have manifested thy name to the men whom thou gavest me out of the world; thine they were, and thou gavest them to me, and they have kept my word. Now they know that everything that thou hast given me is from thee; for I have given them the words which thou gavest me, and they have received them and know in truth that I came from thee; and they have believed that thou didst send me" (John 17:6–8). This was the truth which John wanted the Christians never to dilute. The reason is evident in the next phase of Jesus' priestly prayer for the church which would be born after the resurrection, at Pentecost.

"And now I am no more in the world, but they are in the world, and I am coming to thee. Holy Father, keep them in thy name, which thou hast given me, that they may be one, even as we are one" (John 17:11). Jesus saw his death as the reconciliation of his people to God and to one another. He went to the cross to make us one.

The last portion of Jesus' prayer meant a great deal to John because it dealt directly with the people to whom he wrote in his letter. After Jesus prayed for his disciples, he prayed for those who would believe through the preaching of the Apostles. "I do not pray for these only [the disciples], but also for those who believe in me through their word, that they may be one; even as thou, Father, art in me, and I in thee, that they also may be in us, so that the world may believe that thou hast sent me. The glory which thou hast given me I have given to them, that they may be one even as we are one, I in them and thou in me, that they may become perfectly one, so that the world may know that thou hast sent me and hast loved them even as thou hast loved me" (John 17:20–23).

Surely John had this prayer on his mind as he wrote to the Christians. Now we can see why truth was so important to him. Belief that Jesus was the Son of God and that his word was absolute truth was the first step toward the oneness that Jesus promised. That was irrefragable, incontrovertible. The church was to be the fellowship of people who were one as Jesus and God were one. Amazing! One in truth, one in spirit, one in purpose, one in mutual love. No wonder John was determined to maintain the purity of belief in the incarnation.

In this little letter, with immeasurable concern, John talks about knowing, abiding, and following the truth. The last two define the first. Intellectual comprehension of conceptual truth must be fleshed out in life. Abiding in the truth is internal—in the inner being; following the truth is relational—the moral implication of belief in our relationships.

The words *the truth which abides in us and will be with us forever* mean that the indwelling Christ makes truth the monitor and motivator of our character. The more we focus on Christ, the more we become like him. Our thoughts and emotions are reformed inadvertently. The result is that what we have to share in the fellowship is Christ's love, forgiveness, acceptance, and joy. The Christ in me salutes the Christ in you. We become one in him. This is why there is greater closeness, unity, and enabling freedom in Christ-centered fellowship. It is impossible to experience that with someone who has not allowed Christ, the truth, to abide in him. The point and Person of reference is different. Without Christ indwelling, another person will draw on an altogether different set of values and purposes. There may be a relationship of sorts, but not fellowship.

John goes on to say, "I rejoiced greatly to find some of your children [the members of the congregation] following the truth, just as we have been commanded by the Father." Here is a vital condition to koinonia. Authentic fellowship grows as people in whom Christ the truth dwells follow his guidance together. Oneness of belief instigates unity of direction and goals.

Fellowship in the church does not exist for itself; its life is dependent on movement. We are together in profound mutual love in order to be able to live out our faith in the world. People who have never known the truth and structures of our society which deny or dissemble the truth are the target of the fellowship's agenda.

I am delighted by the quality of "love in truth" fellowship that is growing in our small groups which meet all over Los Angeles. But I am very aware that the strongest groups are those engaged in ministry together. Each individual is held accountable for the way he follows the truth in daily life. Often the whole group will tackle a need in society together. The fellowship is deepened as they pray for and support each other. The members of the group are not together for the warm fuzzies of sharing, Bible study, and prayer, without specific obedience to Christ's example of ministry to individuals and debilitating social problems.

John implies that love in truth is following the Lord's commandments. It's fascinating to note that the Apostle always reasons in a circle when it comes to the subject of the new commandment. Love is the commandment and loving is following the commandment. Christ made that clear. Love for God must be spelled out in love for one another. The quality of love in the fellowship is to liberate us for radical loving in our relationships beyond the fellowship.

That helps us to deal with the levels of relationship which confront all of us. We have friends with whom we share the truth of Christ. These are very satisfying, supportive relationships, where we can be ourselves, love and be loved. But we also live with people in our homes, at work, and in our communities who do not share our conviction or experience of the truth. We should not expect or demand that we have Christian fellowship with them. We are to use the resources of love we have gained in the Christ-centered fellowship to model life in Christ to them.

A man came to me recently to express his disappointment that he did not have true Christian fellowship in his marriage. I asked him about his wife and her belief about the truth. She was a traditional church member, but seemed resistant to a vital encounter with the living Christ. The man's expectation was constantly disappointed. I tried to help him face the reality that until his wife was open to Christ, she would not be open to fellowship. His responsibility was to be Christ's love to her and wait patiently.

Often we demand that a congregation be a deep fellowship without the truth of the gospel as the basic ingredient. I hear church leaders bemoan the lack of love, forgiveness, and closeness among their members. They are constantly looking for some gimmick or program that will produce instant fellowship. The only way to discover that is to preach and teach the exciting new life in Christ and to help the members into a fresh experience of Christ. When he invades these occluded inner hearts and begins to deal with hidden needs and problems, then a new excitement about Christ and the gospel will be born. Then those who are coming alive will find a mutual encouragement and enabling through sharing the difficulties and delights of being Christ's disciples.

Traditional church worship and program usually do not produce fellowship. A winsome, contagious preaching of Christ and his power to change our lives gives birth to a viable life center in the congregation. That is the impelling example which can spread throughout the church.

The subtle forms of Gnosticism still besiege the church today. Whenever people assume that they can make it on their own strength, resist the cross as the only hope for their forgiveness, or deny the need for Christ's intervention in the problematical flesh of our life today, the incarnation is equivocated.

John's second letter has a now-ness about it. It could have been written as a guide for the revival of the church today. The aching need in contemporary church life is a return to the preaching, teaching, living, and sharing of the truth of the incarnation. Any dynamic Christian goes back daily to the amazing grace of what God did and does through Christ. With renewed excitement about that, he is open to honest, truth-oriented fellowship with fellow adventurers.

PRAYER FOR THE DAY: *Lord, we want to focus our whole life on the truth today. Help us to do truth in all our responsibilities. May the truth of your love in the incarnation enable us to be extensions of the incarnation in the challenges and demands of the hours of this day. We open ourselves to the pervading power of your truth about us and our being. Help us to find deep, healing fellowship with those who share the truth. Give us patience and sensitivity with those who do not know the truth. We want to live the truth so vividly that they will want to know the reason for the hope in us. In a world of half-truth and distorted truth, we want to be people who can speak the truth and live it. In your name, and by your power, blessed way, truth, and life! Amen.*

26.

Future Jitters

Grace, mercy, and peace will be with us.

2 John 3

READ: 2 John 3

I awoke with a feeling of anxiety. There was no apparent cause that I could readily identify. It did not go away as I showered, dressed, and ate breakfast. The uneasy mood had increased by the time I reached my study for the day's work. I sat at my desk wondering what was wrong, trying to get in touch with the panic inside me.

In my morning prayer, I asked God to help me. The quiet time finally revealed the cause of the alarm signal ringing in my soul.

Over the previous month I had collected a bag of unresolved problems and potentials. All of them had to wait for solutions, answers from people, and the painfully slow movement of institutional committee machinery. Being a "do it now" and "resolve it today" kind of person makes that excruciating. No amount of pushing, inspiring leadership, or manipulation brought the results I desired. I can usually tolerate a lot of "we'll let you know—don't call us—we'll call you" kinds of situations. But several of these had been coupled with some unfulfilled visions I felt God had put on my agenda. Impatience engulfed me. The build-up finally got to me. For the first time in years, I felt self-doubt. If I were only more adequate or effective or creative, there would be more progress toward the goals I had set. Suddenly I realized that I was anxious about the future. How would things work out? Would there be solutions? What would I do if the dreams didn't come to fruition?

Ever feel that way? Have you experienced a time or times like that? How do you feel about your future? Confident? Patient? Anxious? Uncertain? Panicked?

There are times when we all get hit with a mixed blast of anticipation and worry about the future, often when we least expect it. Our personal or professional future seems to be up for grabs. There may be little concrete evidence that this could be true, but the uneasiness persists. The problem is not in the unknown future circumstances, but inside us.

Though I could not have written it that morning, I can write it now. I'm glad it happened. I have been blessed with a positive, affirmative nature. It's my usual disposition to expect everything to work out in the right way and at the right time. Going through this alarming spasm of emotional frustration has put me in touch with what many people live with every day of their lives. Others face it at crucial passages of their lives. Perhaps you are in one of those times right now as you read this. Maybe someone you love is suffering from "future jitters." So many people I listen to everyday are unable to befriend the future.

That morning when I was being attacked by the virus of future frustrations, my studies were focused in 2 John. Long before I get around to writing a chapter on a biblical passage, I use it for my own devotional reading. That's to let it get at me before I try to get my thoughts into words. My plea for God to help me that morning was answered in the third verse in

John's letter, and it meant so much to me that I have kept
that single verse for a separate chapter of our study.

John's readers were as uncertain of the future as we are at
times. The Apostle's greeting had been written to a church in
Roman Asia, but the Holy Spirit made it a very personal word
for me that morning. It broke the bind and released me to
trust all of my "future jitters" to God.

"Grace, mercy, and peace *will* be with us, from God the
Father and from Jesus Christ the Father's Son, in truth and
love." The future tense leaped off the page. I hadn't seen that
before. Most of the New Testament letters have a salutation
delineating several of the blessings of God. This is the only
one in the future tense. I believe John had more than a cus-
tomary letter-writing nicety in mind; he wanted his beloved
friends to know that the essential gifts of God offered through
Jesus Christ's life, death, and resurrection would be more
than adequate for the unexpected eventualities of the future.
Regardless of what happened to them, grace, mercy and peace
would be their experience.

I want to take you through the experience of this verse that
I had that morning.

First of all, I was deeply moved by the *utter reliability of
the source of the future promise.* God the Father—that would
have been enough. But John adds the superlative, "and from
Jesus Christ the Father's Son." That brought me back to the
incarnation. The One to whom I could trust the future was the
creator, sustainer, redeemer, and Lord of all time and space.
Not bad for openers! Then I began to recount what the birth,
life, death and resurrection of Jesus Christ meant to me personally. I had a Christmas, Easter, and Pentecost celebration
all rolled into one that morning. God had invaded human life
—my life. There was not a problem I could think of that had
not been dealt with in the Master's message.

His death had been a "once for all" forgiveness of my sins.
That helped me realize that fear of the future is really fear of
failure. If all that I was planning and pushing did not work

out, I was free to accept the failure in the warm assurance of the Lord's forgiveness. That gave me renewed daring and confidence—now not in myself, but in him.

A reminder of the Resurrection gave me hope. I remembered the Lord's promise, "Because I live you *shall* live also." If death has been defeated, what did I have to fear? I am alive forever. The brief days of this life are pitifully short in comparison to eternity. Added to that, resurrection is the promise of God not only when we die but when we "die daily," as Paul put it. The death of our worrisome wish-dreams is always followed by the resurrection of an unexpected intervention from the Lord. When we let go of our tomorrows he gives us confidence in our todays. I felt that as I studied and prayed that morning.

Pentecost followed. I reaffirmed my privilege of being a recipient of this climax of the historic incarnation. The resurrected Christ is the indwelling Spirit. My future jitters were a gift to let me know that my greatest need was for a fresh filling of the Spirit. I was reminded of something I have taught and preached to others. The Holy Spirit gives us gifts for each new opportunity or challenge. We cannot store them up as a permanent endowment. They are given as equipment for effective ministry—daily, momentarily. Preparation for the future is a present, personal relationship with the Giver of the gifts. With that assurance, I could hear the Lord say, "Give me your tomorrows. . . ." The day and the way would be given.

My mind drifted over the thirty years I have lived in the new life in Christ. I thought of his perfectly timed strategy in my life. Always on time! The churches I served, the movements in which I had been involved, my marriage, my wife's healing of cancer, the years raising the children, the serendipities in daily problems—the Lord had never failed to give me what I needed. But never ahead of time. I felt the tight spring of tension unwind inside me. It was as if the Lord himself peeled off the fingers of my autocratic grip on the future. His words in my inner being were piercing. He wanted my abdication from trying to run the universe. The utter reliability of the source of John's promise had changed my mood.

I was now ready to appropriate *the absolute availability of the substance* of the Apostle's magnificent greeting. Grace, mercy, and peace. I contemplated the unresolved problems that had overloaded the circuits of my emotions. If I could be sure that each of them would be an opportunity to experience fresh grace, mercy, and peace, all would be well.

I turned each of the three words over in my mind. Then I discovered a new insight. There is a progression in these words. One follows the other irrevocably. Grace is God's unchanging nature; mercy is his nature applied to our needs; and peace is his nature in us. We can be sure that God's grace, his unmerited favor toward us, is as predictable as the sunrise. He will not deny or contradict himself. We can count on that. His mercy is involved, identifying love. He will be in the situations we fear in the future. By his providence, all things will work together for our good and his plan. Peace settles in our hearts when we really believe that.

I had not thought of it before. Grace, mercy, and peace are special gifts for the three aspects of our nature. Grace can be contemplated. We can think about what God is. Mercy is experienced in our emotions. We feel loved and that love casts out fear and anxiety. Peace is volitional. We receive it only after we have surrendered our wills to do God's will at all costs. The only way to deal with tomorrow is to accept all three gifts today: to meditate on his grace, to let him mercifully love us, and to give him complete control in exchange for an abiding peace.

Paul was on target: "Right now God is ready to welcome you. Today he is ready to save you" (2 Cor. 6:2, TLB). Knowing that we can look forward to tomorrow. It will be exciting to see how the Lord will use everything to break through with grace to sustain us, mercy to encourage us, and peace to comfort us. His promise is sure: "Lo, I am with you always"

(Matt. 28:20). "Don't be anxious about tomorrow. God will take care of your tomorrow too. Live one day at a time" (Matt. 6:34, TLB). That's all I needed to know! My future jitters had been healed.

PRAYER FOR THE DAY: *Dear Lord of the future, we praise you that you know what you are doing with our tomorrows. We confidently anticipate each new day and expectantly await the discovery of your grace, mercy, and peace in all of our unresolved problems and potentials. We believe that everything that will happen to us will be used for your plan and purpose. Thank you for healing our future jitters. Amen.*

27.

When Tolerance Is a Tragedy

For many deceivers have gone out into the world, men who will not acknowledge the coming of Jesus Christ in the flesh.

2 John 7

READ: 2 John 7–13

"Well, the least we can do is to be tolerant!" The woman's exclamation was meant to be magnanimous. In a way, she was right. Tolerance is the *least* we can do. Often, it's the very least!

We live in a time when tolerance has been made the crown of the attitudinal virtues. It's been an important antidote to prejudice. We've been taught to be tolerant of other people's beliefs, ideas, and backgrounds. But mere tolerance alone is ineffective when it comes to really caring about people and taking them seriously.

Nobody wants to be tolerated. We all want more than indulgence of our convictions or life-style. Aloof toleration communicates lack of esteem and value. Who wants people simply to endure our differences or uniqueness?

Some of us hide behind the simplistic, sentimental assertion that it doesn't make any difference what a person believes.

We say that everybody has a right to believe whatever he wants. Sounds lovely, doesn't it?

But when does concern for a person give us the right to confront him about belief which may rob him of a full and abundant life? And what if that person is actively promulgating debilitating beliefs to others? Is it our responsibility to battle for truth? Can toleration go too far?

John's answer would be a resounding "Yes!" His second letter, from verse 7 on, seems to be very intolerant of the Gnostic defectors from the faith and the fellowship of the church. John not only cautioned the Christians to see them as deceivers and the antichrist, but urged them to expose and resist the heretical doctrine they taught.

At first, the words of the Apostle of Love seem harsh and strangely inconsistent with his constantly repeated admonition that we should love one another. Is there a contradiction here? Shouldn't love enable the members of the church to be tolerantly accepting regardless of what the Gnostics said or did? We wonder about John's instruction not to receive them into the house or give them any greeting. Have we caught the Apostle in a weakness—an inability to express love to certain people? Is there a limit to the quality of love he's written about so much?

John has shown us that there is a time when authentic love makes us intolerant. It was out of *agapē* love that he became very protective of the purity of the church. He knew that if the Gnostic heresy continued to spread virulently in the church, the future ministry would be crippled. Added to that, the Apostle cared enough about the Gnostics themselves not to trifle with their divisive activities. They had adopted beliefs which negated their eternal life, then and forever. Toleration would be tacit approval. For him it would be as unloving as standing by while a person drank poison.

As we have seen in 1 John 4:2–3, the Gnostics denied the reality of the incarnation. They did not believe that Jesus was the Christ and actually had dwelt in the flesh. In this second

letter there is a shift in the tense of the participle which makes
the situation even more intolerable. "For many deceivers have
gone out into the world, men who will not acknowledge the
coming of Jesus Christ in the flesh." The present middle tense
of the participle stresses the continuing incarnation. John is
alarmed not only that they did not accept that Jesus Christ
came, but that he comes. The issue at stake was the continuing reality of the incarnation.

The denial of the historic incarnation of God in Jesus of
Nazareth, the Messiah, eventually leads to a denial of his influence and intervention in our daily life. If God who is spirit
and therefore good could not enter into flesh which was evil,
how could he have any contact or concern for our life in the
flesh? The Gnostic god was separated from the real world.
They held to rigid dichotomy between good and evil, spirit
and matter, God and the flesh. That not only negated the incarnation, cross and redemption, it resulted in a kind of heresy
which denied the power of the Holy Spirit to enter into Christians' lives and transform their humanity. You be the judge:
should John and the church members tolerate that fallacious
distortion of truth?

Actually, the Gnostics were very intolerant of the Christians. They were constantly trying to dissuade the members of
the church from the central truth of the gospel. Infiltrating
the church, they tried to weaken the belief in the incarnation
from within the Body of Christ. They claimed an advanced,
more highly refined brand of Christianity. That's what John
was referring to in verse 9: "Anyone who goes ahead and does
not abide in the doctrine of Christ does not have God; he who
abides in the doctrine of Christ has both the Father and the
Son." The Greek word for "goes ahead" is *proagōn,* meaning
to go out in advance. The false teachers claimed that they
were the progressive thinkers and that the Christians were
backward in their dependence on the doctrine of the incarnation. John was for progress and creative advance, but always
based on the essential truth that God came in the flesh and

comes into the raw reality of life daily and momentarily. The Gnostic theosophy, which claimed a new mystical, and esoteric insight about God, made Jesus one of a series of emanations from God. This was not advanced thinking at all. It was an old idea that had been around for a long time among the Greeks. John called for direct confrontation of their intolerant attitude.

We are taken back by the Apostle's radical advice to the Christians on how to deal with the false teachers. "If anyone comes to you and does not bring this doctrine, do not receive him into the house or give him any greeting; for he who greets him shares his wicked work" (vv. 10–11).

My first reaction is to object to John's severity. How could the Christians have any influence on the Gnostics if they refused to have anything to do with them? Wouldn't it have been better to develop trusting relationships with them in order to be able to lead them back to the truth?

John saw the situation in emergency dimensions. The confusing teachers were after the jugular vein of Christianity. They had to be shocked into a realization that their teaching was false and would destroy the church.

When John says, "Do not receive them into the house," he is talking about the fellowship of the church which met in a particular home. The impact is: don't allow the philosophers to be a part of the church; don't give them a platform to speak their distorted theories; don't confuse potential converts to the faith with the idea that Gnosticism is a legitimate expression of Christianity.

The greeting John says should be withheld is the greeting of peace which was exchanged between Christians. Perhaps the "kiss of peace" is implied. It would be completely incongruous to greet a person in the name of Christ who did not believe that he was the incarnate Word of God. The defectors were trying to pretend to be part of Christianity in order to win the Christians over to their ideas. That's why there could be no compromise with them.

What does all this mean to us? Plenty! We are living in a time when contemporary manifestations of the same problem faces the church and Christians. We are confronted with both blatant and subtle denials of the incarnation in the church. Leaders and members within the Christian community evade the centrality of Jesus Christ and the incarnation. He is presented as the best of good men, but not as the Savior and the only way to God. Or the teachings of Christ are used as the basis of psychological insight without the necessity of accepting Christ as Lord of our lives. He is taught as one of many ways to God. The problem of sin as separation from God is evaded. The cross is sentimentalized. The necessity for conversion is neglected and the new birth is overlooked. All in the name of Christianity!

Many groups that openly deny the incarnation as the central touchstone of Christianity want to be called a church. Often it's for tax purposes. More often it's a desire to use a semblance of church life to lead people away from historic Christianity. Scientology is one of the most dangerous offenders. In Los Angeles, it is one of the most militant movements seeking to lead young people away from basic trust of Christ as only Savior and Lord. Throughout the nation there is an upsurge of cults and "new thought" movements. Many claim to be a brand of Christianity while blending the gospel with Eastern religions, meditation, and self-help psychology.

But by far the greatest concern is Christians who deny the gospel by the basic assumption of culturalized Christianity. Among our friends are those who believe that God only helps those who help themselves; that we can syncretize Christ and our passion for material security; and that we are loved by God because we are good, honest, or industrious. The radical nature of the incarnation is denied in our refusal to see ourselves as sinners in need of forgiveness. The contemporary brand of Gnosticism is expressed by those who hold to the customs of the Christian year, including Christmas, Easter, and Pentecost, without a personal experience of Christ today. The test is not only that Christ lived, but that he lives today—in us and as Lord of history.

The astounding phenomenon of our time is the great numbers of church members who are discovering a personal relationship with Christ for the first time. Church people are coming alive! The Christ who came continues to come to incarnate the reality of his birth, death, resurrection, and indwelling power in people today. Someone went beyond bland toleration to tell them what they were missing.

John has challenged us to love profoundly enough to do more than tolerate people. We should recognize the danger of false teaching and thinking. Confrontation is an expression of love. No one is helped by superficial acceptance that does not grapple with basic presuppositions. We are called to engage people in serious discussion about what they believe. When the basic beliefs of the church are in peril, we must love enough to raise the standard of the authority of Scripture and the irreducible maximum of the incarnation as the central fact of history and as our only hope today.

A brilliant man who recently became a Christian expressed the point dramatically. "I am very thankful that you kept after me. You listened to all my philosophic ramblings with patience, but not tolerance. You cared enough to meet me point for point, idea for idea. You took my struggle seriously. I would never have become a Christian if I had not felt that you were absolutely convinced that Christ was the only answer for your life . . . and that I was lost without him. If I could have driven a wedge in that conviction, or if you had let me off the hook with some kind of equivocation, I would not have kept searching."

There are people like this man in the lives of all of us. The Lord has put them in our sphere of influence because he loves them. Our love for them must be decisive and penetrating. If they know we care, they will respond to our desire to share what we've discovered. It is for each of us to find ways of raising questions, challenging values, and showing people what a difference Christ has made in our lives. Uninvolved toleration is not love at all!

PRAYER FOR THE DAY: *Dear God, thank you for not tolerating the sin of the world. Because you cared, you came in Jesus Christ to reconcile us to yourself. You did not tolerate our rebellion, but invaded us with love and forgiveness. Give us the courage to do more than tolerate people. Help us to remember what life was like before we knew you personally. May that shock us out of bland aloofness from the peril in which people around us are living. Thank you for giving us joy and hope to share. In the quiet of this moment, clarify for us the people in our lives who have been prepared by you for a loving and decisive confrontation. Through the Christ who came and comes. Amen.*

28.

Gracious Living

*The Elder to beloved Gaius, whom I love in the truth.
. . . But Diotrephes, who likes to put himself first . . . .*

3 John 1, 9

READ: 3 John 1–10

The advertisement held out quite a promise. "Discover gracious living in these magnificent condominiums!" As if gracious living could be acquired by moving into a $200,000 condominium, the sellers went on to talk about pleasant surroundings and an affluent ambience. That started me thinking about what gracious living really is.

Perhaps that was the reason that a Thanksgiving Day ad by a local restaurant caught my eye. "Spend A Gracious Thanksgiving Day With Us." I thought of people away from home or without a home who might take up the offer. Then I pictured some homes in which Thanksgiving Day celebrations would be anything but gracious.

With that on my mind, I was particularly sensitive to a comment a woman made as she was leaving church: "Thanks for being a gracious church!" I stopped her to ask what she meant. "Well," she replied, "I felt accepted and welcomed.

Even though I was staggered by the size of the congregation, I felt the service was just for me. The people around me in the sanctuary made me feel important and significant, as if I had been a member here all my life!"

I was gratified by this reaffirmation that two sermons were preached that Sunday: one by the preacher and the other by the congregation in the pew. One of the greatest challenges for the local church is for its life to be congruent with its spoken message. An effective tool of church growth evangelism is the quality of the fellowship.

What is gracious living? What makes us gracious persons to others? How can our churches be gracious congregations? These questions were tumbling around in my mind like laundry in a clothes dryer when I reread the third of John's letters to the churches. His plea was for graciousness. The comparison of two very different personalities, Gaius and Diotrephes, clarifies what gracious living for a Christian is all about. 3 John is an encouragement for the church to practice hospitality.

The letter is addressed to Gaius. Who was he? There are three Gaiuses in the New Testament. Gaius of Corinth was Paul's host. He refers to him with admiration in Romans 16: 23. Then there was Gaius of Derbe who carried a collection for the poor to Jerusalem, recorded in Acts 20:4. A third Gaius is by far the best choice. He was the Macedonian who was entangled in the riot in Ephesus over the conflict between the Christian and the silversmiths. He was clearly identified with Paul and was one of his faithful followers. His commitment to Christ was galvanized by persecution. Tradition has it that he was made the bishop of the church at Pergamum, one of the churches to receive John's letters. The geographical proximity, coupled with Gaius's experience and growth in Christ in Roman Asia, convinces me that he was the same man addressed in the opening of this third letter.

John says some remarkable things about Gaius and his

leadership. We feel the depth of Christian intimacy expressed in their friendship. All that John has taught about the closeness and warmth of true koinonia in Christ is exemplified in the way he writes to Gaius and what he says about him.

In the first two verses of the letter John refers to Gaius as "beloved." The greek word is drenched with meaning. Rooted in the *agapē* quality of love John has used to distinguish God's love, it is giving and forgiving, unchanging and unlimited, unmotivated by our deserving and unqualified by our performance. John loves Gaius with that kind of love. *Beloved* is the word of endearment of Christian intimacy. It communicates delight, appreciation, and admiration. Most of all, *beloved* carries the precious cargo of shared hopes and dreams as well as mutual experience for profound forgiveness and assurance. We are *agapētōi* (beloved) to each other when we have found *agapē* together. That quality of gracious relationship must be grown in the rich soil of shared truth as well as feeling. Then John wrote "to the beloved Gaius, whom I love in the truth." We all have to be of one mind as well as one heart with others who share the adventure of following the Master. John had stressed that in the second letter.

Agapē love has a gracious quality of caring. John wants to know how his beloved friend Gaius is doing. He tells him that he is praying that all is well with him. Note that his prayers are for his physical as well as spiritual life. Graciousness is wholistic: it is concerned about a person's emotional, physical, and relational life.

A man expressed the problem of our busy lives today. "Who cares any more, really?" he demanded. A long series of shattering experiences had brought the man to his shocking question.

Gaius cared and enabled a church of caring people. Word had come to John about Gaius's church. He had been told that Gaius's faithfulness in preaching and teaching Christ had paid off in the development of a gracious congregation. The people were living the truth in their relationships with each other. "No greater joy can I have than this," writes John, "to hear that my children follow the truth" (v. 4).

When the gospel is vividly proclaimed, the objective truth of God's love in the cross produces a subjective expression in the people's attitude toward each other. Recently the deacons of our church adopted the basic purpose of caring for the congregation, so that the people would learn to care for each other, so that then we could all care about the world Christ died to save. That left me and my fellow pastors with the challenge to care for the deacons so they could accomplish this purpose. Gaius is our guide.

He helped his people to do "a loyal thing" (v. 5), a faith-filled work. They rendered service not only to the fellow members of the church, but to strangers. Matthew 25:35 tolls in our minds. Jesus said, "I was a stranger and you welcomed me. . . ." We are quick to join the disciples' quickened query, "When did we see thee a stranger and welcome thee?" The Lord's disturbing response was that in the stranger they would meet him and what they would do to welcome the stranger they would do for him. Gaius's church had become distinguished throughout the province for its welcome and service to strangers.

Hospitality is practical graciousness. It's the "open heart and home" expression of love. The New Testament epistles are filled with admonitions about the obligation of Christian hospitality. Paul challenged the Christians at Rome to "practice hospitality" (Rom. 12:13); Peter said, "Practice hospitality ungrudgingly to one another" (1 Pet. 4:9). The letter to the Hebrews goes deeper in suggesting that strangers may be vistors from the Lord: "Do not neglect to show hospitality to strangers, for thereby some have entertained angels unawares" (Heb. 13:2). An angel is a messenger from God. The meaning for us today is that God does bless us by sending us people who can enrich our lives, but also, who give us the opportunity to actualize our love by caring for their needs. In our giving we are blessed more than the stranger who receives. When Paul delineated the qualifications of a bishop, hospitality was listed along with such qualities as faithfulness to one wife, temperance, sensibleness, dignity, ability to teach, and freedom from drunkenness, violence, quarrelsomeness, and love of money (1 Tim. 3:2–3). In the light of that, we can appreciate why he wanted Titus to be "a lover of hospitality" (Tit. 1:8).

John was particularly commendatory of Gaius's hospitable church not only because non-Christian strangers were welcomed and introduced to Christ, but also because his congregation was a gracious way-station for the traveling itinerant preachers, prophets, and missionaries who were reaching the pagan world outside the church. Gaius's people made these wandering adventurers welcome, ministered to their personal needs, and sent them on their mission replenished physically and spiritually. Here was a missionary congregation in the first century. They were not so concerned about the welfare of their own local fellowship that they could not support the expansion of Christianity. Gaius and his congregation saw one mission that included what God was doing in their church and beyond in the world. Not all of them were called to be missionaries, but their love and support involved them in the missionary enterprise of the church.

Churches today grapple with the demands of local church ministry and the responsibility of supporting the expansion of Christianity around the globe. Often the two become competitive rather than complementary aspects of one mission. Dynamic congregations become and remain strong only so long as they reach out to the spiritual and social needs of the city, nation, and world. A part of the death rattle in a congregation's demise is introverted self-concern which spends all its money and energy on its own building and program. Prayer, sacrifical giving, in-depth understanding and vital involvement in mission can resurrect a church. A spiritual law is involved. A congregation exists for what happens beyond its own doors. Any local church which believes and practices that law soon finds that what happens behind its doors is an explosion of power and effectiveness.

Not everyone believes that. Some become defensive of the local church and its authority. Diotrephes would be a petulant patron of localism. He opposed Gaius's open door and heart policy. His diatribe against outsiders, including John, won him a place in Scripture—last place. He is remembered as one who refused to welcome strangers, support the missionaries, and submit to the wisdom of leaders of the church.

Background is helpful. By the end of the first century, an ordered authority had emerged. Local congregations were led by elders called forth and ordained from among the people. Diotrephes was probably one of these church officers. Gaius seems to have had broader leadership over a city or area. The itinerant preachers were given an even wider realm of responsibility and went from congregation to congregation preaching the gospel. They were like traveling missionaries. Above all of them was John, whose authority was rooted in his apostleship. He had been a part of the original band of Jesus' disciples, had witnessed the crucifixion and resurrection, and had been instrumental in the expansion of the infant church. Diotrephes's problem was that he did not want to take direction or wisdom from anyone. He considered his church his own private domain.

His imperiousness was nurtured by a spiritual malignancy. John diagnosed it. Diotrephes "likes to put himself first." That's why he could not acknowledge John's authority or accept the help of the itinerants. His "I'll do it myself " arrogance led to a "keep your hands off my church!" kind of independence. Diotrephes was ambitious and competitive. He longed for glory and recognition. An aching insecurity which he had never allowed Christ to heal made him testy and divisive. Nothing seemed to satisfy his expansive ego. Driven by the wrong reasons, he committed spiritual treason. He took on none other than the Aspostle John, refusing to allow his letters to be read to his congregation. 2 John is implied. By the fact that that letter was a forthright condemnation of Gnosticism, we are led to agree with such biblical scholars as A. T. Robertson that Diotrephes probably was a Gnostic sympathizer and one of the dangerous leaders who were drawing the church astray into a syncretism of heresy and Christianity. His name *Dios* and *trephō*, meaning nourished by Zeus,[1] suggests a pagan background. The problem was that he was nourished by a very poisonous, aggressive passion to be in charge. He majored in the disputation of minutiae and got his congregation away from the purpose of being an inclusive, contagious, Christ-centered fellowship of believers.

John puts it straight: He is "prating against me with evil words. And not content with that, he refuses to welcome the brethren, and also stops those who want to welcome them and puts them out of the church" (3 John 10). Theological debate was a smoke screen for his unstable relationship with Christ. At taproot, his heart was polluted. It's not so much the love of truth which keeps people apart as our distorted love of ourselves.

Again, as in the second letter, John shows us that confrontation is a part of graciousness. He sees Diotrephes for what he is and plans to confront him when he visits the church. It takes a great measure of love to face a person and settle differences directly. We often think of graciousness as easy-going pleasantness. True graciousness is tough, incisive, and honest. Love is too precious to be diluted in irresponsible joviality. John really cares about Diotrephes and what he is doing to his church. His diatribe would be met with dynamic accountability!

We are left to wonder if the reason we are often ungracious

---

[1] A. T. Robertson, *Word Pictures in the New Testament, The General Epistles and the Revelation of John,* vol. 6 (Nashville, Tenn.: Broadman Press, 1933), p. 263.

is because we have hidden feelings about people which hinder our love and concern. Neglect is eloquent rejection.

Gracious living is life in the flow of Jesus' Spirit. It is a life of freedom and joy because we are offered more than adequate resources for each day. Companionship with him reproduces his life and love through us. But John always gives us a reassuring focus to evaluate our experience of what he teaches us. Hospitality is the outward expression of a gracious person.

A young theological student asked his pastor, "How am I doing?" "Doing what?" was the honest reply, indicative of the student's inactivity in expressing gracious hospitality to people in need of healing love. The insensitive diminutive Diotrephes was too busy fighting theological battles and criticizing his opponents to get on with the main business of life.

The crucial question is not *how* am I doing but *what* am I doing!

PRAYER FOR THE DAY: *Gracious God, you have shown us what authentic graciousness is. We want to live this day as gracious persons. You have made us hosts for the strangers of the world. We commit the hours of this day to hospitality. Flow through our words and actions as we meet people who are strangers because of their strangeness with you. We offer an open heart to welcome them in your name. Amen.*

29.

Ah Demetrius!

Demetrius has testimony from every one, and from the truth itself.

3 John 12

READ: 3 John 11–12

A single verse captures the drama of the transformation of a personality. A passing reference ushers us into a life story. John mentions a person by the name of Demetrius who has a threefold testimony of the authenticity of his commitment to Christ: from everyone, from the truth itself, and from John himself. Quite a recommendation! Who is this Demetrius and what does his life tell us about the intimate life of power John so eloquently describes in his letters?

I believe that this Demetrius was none other than the silversmith of Ephesus who was the leader of the opposition to Paul when he preached the gospel in that Vanity Fair of the Roman province of Asia. Acts 19 tells about him. "There arose no little stir concerning the Way [Christianity]. For a man named Demetrius, a silversmith, who made silver shrines of Artemis, brought no little business to the craftsmen" (vv. 23–24).

These small models of the temple, which would be purchased at great price and set up in homes, had a statue of Artemis, the goddess of fertility, inside. The temple built in her
honor in Ephesus was considered one of the seven wonders of
the then-known world. Her statue, which dominated the
temple, was a many-breasted figure which was believed to
have fallen from the heavens. In May each year a festival was
held to worship Artemis, and this was the business rush of the
year for the silversmiths. Religion and patriotism blended together to produce a sellers' market with great profit for the
silversmiths; that is, until Christianity invaded Ephesus and
the church began to grow with power and hundreds of converts. Paul's teaching of salvation through Christ alone had
made the idolatry of Artemis worship unthinkable and forbid-
den for the followers of the Way.

No wonder Demetrius organized a riot against the Christians! He had probably organized the trade union and
provided the capital for the business. He was not just concerned about the silversmiths, but his own investment.

The picture of Demetrius before his conversion is alarming.
Luke quotes him in Acts as a very dangerous organizer of the
vested interest. He is portrayed as a very clever instigator of
violence. Listen to him speak in Acts 19:25–27: "Men, you
know that from this business we have our wealth. And you see
and hear that not only at Ephesus but almost throughout all
Asia this Paul has persuaded and turned away a considerable
company of people, saying that gods made with hands are not
gods. And there is danger not only that this trade of ours may
come into disrepute but also that the temple of the great goddess Artemis may count for nothing, and that she may even be
deposed from her magnificence, she whom all Asia and the
world worship."

A riot resulted from that inciting speech. Ephesus was filled
with confusion and leaders of the church, Gaius among them,
were dragged into the city theater and beaten. The crowd,

drugged with an economic overdose of fear and frenzy, chanted, "Great is Artemis of the Ephesians."

The Christians would surely have been martyred, and eventually Paul with them, if it had not been for a wise and conciliatory town clerk who quieted the mob and dismissed the riot: "If therefore Demetrius and the craftsmen with him have a complaint against any one, the courts are open, and there are proconsuls; let them bring charges against one another. But if you seek anything further [about these matters], it shall be settled in the regular assembly" (Acts 19: 38–39).

That's all we hear about Demetrius in the New Testament until this reference by John at the close of his third letter. We wonder what happened to bring him to Christ and to the laudable level of Christian maturity John extols.

Tradition has suggested that he was converted to Christ and became a leader of the peripatetic bands of preachers who spread the gospel throughout the area. If this is true, the transformation of his values, priorities, and character must have been an astounding witness to the life-reorienting power of Christ. Many believe that he was the bearer of these letters from John to the churches. A man who was more concerned about money than truth and who led the movement against Christ in Ephesus became an admired and trusted communicator of the gospel.

We feel the triumphant transition which Christ enabled in the life of Demetrius when we consider the amazing recommendation John gives him. There must have been a motive for this commendation. Perhaps Demetrius was a target of one of Diotrephes' diatribes against the wandering prophets of the early church. To balance the scales of judgment and hostility, John places the weight of a threefold accolade. Everyone, says John, testifies to the evidence of the gospel in Demetrius's life. Further, the truth itself is exhibited in his life. Demetrius fulfills John's qualification of "doing the truth" mentioned in the opening of the first letter. Finally, John puts his own life and reputation on the line for Demetrius. No reader of the letter would question the word of the respected Apostle of Love. We feel the warmth of John's feelings for Demetrius.

The Apostle's strong affirmation of Demetrius is a very specific illustration of his admonition in verse 11: "Beloved, do not imitate evil but imitate good. He who does good is of God; he who does evil has not seen God." John implies the contrast of those who resist specific loving and those who have testified for Demetrius. God always personalizes love in a person who needs our help and uplifting assurance.

You are probably wondering why I have taken this much space to tell the story of the transformation of a single personality. The reason is quite simple: I want us to identify with Demetrius and to identify the Demetriuses of our life.

Demetrius's metamorphosis may seem too spectacular for us. And yet, it does force us to question what changes in our habits, attitudes, character, and personality have been the result of intimacy with Christ. What are the identifiable signs that we are new creatures in Christ? The best test of that may be to ask the people with whom we live and work!

Some of us have not had a radical conversion with an observable black-and-white, night-and-day change in our personalities. We may not have been a convert from Black Pantherism like Eldridge Cleaver, from opportunism like Charles Colson, or from violent murder like Tex Watson. But what difference has Christ made for us?

The reason some of us are reluctant to witness to what Christ has done to transform our personalities is that we still see so much of the old person dominating our actions and reactions. But we need not be timid; we are in transition. We belong to Christ and he is at work in us, molding us into the persons we were meant to be.

Perhaps our honest admission that we are far from perfect is our point of contact with people who are struggling to discover what Christ could mean to them. It's when we can share with them what Christ is doing in our personal lives—our marriages, jobs, self-esteem, and hopes—that we can help them feel what Christ could do for them.

This passage from John's letter has given me a reflective pause for reevaluation. I hope it will do the same for you. John has involved us in an inventory of what Christ has accomplished in our personalities. That's reason for gratitude and praise. But we all will be able to see areas which have not been brought under Christ's control. And that's reason for deeper commitment and surrender! Before you read on, list out what aspects of your personality contradict your commitment to Christ. What has he had to say about your relationships? Now, consider your lifestyle. What are the next steps of obedience for you? Remember that John's test of intimacy with Christ is Christlikeness and costly love for people.

Such a time of honest evaluation leads me back to one of my favorite verses from Paul's letter to the Philippians: "Not that I have already obtained this or am already perfect; but I press on to make it my own, because Christ Jesus has made me his own. Brethren, I do not consider that I have made it my own; but one thing I do, forgetting what lies behind and straining forward to what lies ahead, I press on toward the goal for the prize of the upward call of God in Christ Jesus" (Phil. 3:12–14).

But what about the Demetriuses in our lives? John laid his life on the line for Demetrius. Peter befriended Mark at the deepest time of the young missionary's failure and brought him back to effectiveness for Christ. Paul, who was often incisive in his judgments, staked his reputation on the personality transformation of Onesimus, a converted runaway slave, whom he called a "faithful and beloved brother" when commending him to the Colossians and his former owner, Philemon.

The fabric of the Christian fellowship is woven together with the threads of mutual affirmation. And yet, that fabric is more often torn apart by negative criticism, gossip, and thoughtless analysis of others. It's difficult for people to overcome failures or battle compulsive patterns and make a fresh start; most of us are unwilling to be as gracious to them as Christ has been to us.

I am convinced that an acid test of our commitment to Christ is that we have one or several Demetriuses for whom we are expressing remedial and reconciling love. There are always more than enough Diotrepheses around whose criticism is rooted in deeper issues of self-interest and prejudice. We ought to be known for the fact that we are helping transformed people to find acceptance and love, as well as a chance to be productive and creative. Paul gives us the bench mark: "From now on, therefore, we regard no one from a human point of view." Suspicion of a person's past performance is to be overcome with forgiveness and acceptance.

Ah Demetrius! We all have the same needs under the surface. If the truth were known, we would need your affirmation as much as you need ours. We have all been where you are, needing to be befriended and encouraged. We would not do less for you than we have had done for us . . . and may need again before this day is finished!

PRAYER FOR THE DAY: *Lord, help us to identify the Demetriuses in our lives. We know that in the way we relate to them we are relating to you. Make us aware of the inner cowardice which keeps us from affirming your new life in people. May the realization of the unmerited favor of your grace in our lives soften our judgments and overcome our suspicions. You have always been for us when we deserved it the least; how can we do less for others? You have given us countless new beginnings. We praise you for this day's opportunities to open doors of opportunity for others. In your viable Name. Amen.*

30.

The Gift of Peace

Peace be to you.

3 John 15

READ: 3 John 15

Try to get in touch with your inner feelings. Do you have a deep, abiding sense of peace inside? Can you remember when you did? How did it feel? If you had to write a definition of peace, what would it be?

Now be very honest with yourself. Do you know what robs you of peace? What has the power to unsettle you? To make you feel uneasy, insecure, fragmented, at loose ends? You know what it is or who it is. Past memories, present pressures, future uncertainties. Things unfinished, broken relationships, self-condemnation. How would you like to give up the broken pieces of your life and allow God to give you an unbreakable peace?

John ends his third letter with a gift: "Peace be to you." This was more than a familiar parting word; it expressed John's deepest longing for his friends. But most of all, it summarized all that he had tried to communicate in all three letters. If John's friends took seriously what he had said, they would have peace.

Writing this book has been more than an exercise in exposition for me. I have pictured you, the reader. A friendship has developed in my heart for you. I have felt that I was sharing inner hopes with a close, trusted friend. All during the hours of writing, I have prayed that you would understand and respond. The result is that I now can share with John the urgency of wanting you to know peace. If I could give you a gift of love, it would be the gift of peace. I know how short life is. And yet, it is so often jangled with problems which beset us and keep us on edge.

An inner voice within me sounds a caution. Be careful, Lloyd. You want to give your reader the gift of peace. Do you know what that requires? Peace is the result of healing, wholeness, and the power of the Holy Spirit.

Suddenly I am less glib; much more empathetic. I feel the pulsebeat of God himself when he yearned over Israel. "They have healed the wound of my people lightly, saying, 'Peace, peace,' when there is no peace. . . . Is there no balm in Gilead? Is there no physician there? Why then has the health of my people not been restored?" (Jer. 8:11,20). Whenever I get in touch with people, the struggles they endure, and the false peace that is offered by so many, I say, "Peace be to you!" with a greater appreciation of not only the need, but the cost, of the gift I would offer.

Let's consider this word *peace*. What does it mean? How is it experienced? How can we share it with others?

It's interesting that the word *peace* is both a greeting and parting blessing throughout the Scriptures. In Hebrew it is captured in the single word *shalom*. In Greek it's *eirēnē soi;* in Latin, *pax tibi*. Whichever language, the intention is the same. Peace is the legacy of Christ. All that he said, did, and does is to enable peace in our hearts.

On the night before Jesus was crucified, he gave the bequest of peace which his crucifixion and resurrection would actualize in his disciples. "Peace I leave with you; my peace I give to you; not as the world gives do I give to you. Let not your hearts be troubled, neither let them be afraid" (John 14: 27). These words were fraught with new meaning when a few days later the resurrected Lord appeared to the disciples and greeted them, *"Shalom!"* Their shattered hearts experienced peace when they knew he was alive. But deeper inner peace was the result of Pentecost when he took up residence in their hearts.

The adventuresome years that followed were filled with inner peace in the midst of conflict and persecution. The Apostle found that Jesus' peace was greater than the world could offer or try to deny. The peace Jesus provided encompassed the full meaning of the word. Peace is the knitting together of what is raveled or broken.

Peace is the result of clarified priorities. Any consideration of the meaning of peace must come to terms with Jesus' very disturbing clarification of the kind of peace he offers. "Do not think that I have come to bring peace on earth; I have not come to bring peace, but a sword. For I have come to set a man against his father, and a daughter against her mother, and a daughter-in-law against her mother-in-law; and a man's foes will be those of his own household. He who loves father or mother more than me is not worthy of me; and he who loves son or daughter more than me is not worthy of me; and he who does not take up his cross and follow me is not worthy of me. He who finds his life will lose it, and he who loses his life for my sake will find it" (Matt. 10:34–39).

Well! Peace is not a gentle, sentimental thing after all. Jesus demands absolute loyalty and commitment to him. There can be no conflicting loyalty to family, friends, or our ambitions for our lives to get in the way of following him. Second place is one place he will not accept.

The absence of peace in our hearts may be the alarming sign that something or someone has moved into first place. We cannot serve two masters—Christ and anyone else—not even ourselves! If there is little peace in us right now, the cause may be that we have confused our priorities and broken the first commandment. Our goals, positions, the people of our lives, and our symbols of security can become false gods. Peace is the outgrowth of giving Christ first priority. We can say, "Peace be to you!" but it will have no meaning until we loose our tight grip on the people and things through which we are trying to gain the uneasy semblance of peace.

Next, peace is the result of forgiveness of ourselves and others. Memories! The memory of failure can rub our consciences raw and deny us peace. We cannot have the peace of God until we are at peace with God. That means seeking forgiveness for what we have said and done. The necessary outgrowth of that will be the freedom to forgive ourselves. We all need the assurance that we are right with God and ourselves. Then we can forgive others. Oliver Cromwell said that if we are to have a peace without a worm in it, we must lay the foundation of righteousness and justice. That requires cleaning the slate of past sins and extending to others what has been given to us. D. L. Moody was decisive about peace: "A great many people are trying to make peace, but that has already been done. God has not left it to us to do; all we have to do is enter into it."

Entering the peace of God is accepting what he has offered through Christ and then appropriating it for others in our attitude and acceptance. Paul captured the wonder of it all: "For in him [Christ] all the fulness of God was pleased to dwell, and through him to reconcile to himself all things, whether on earth or in heaven, making peace by the blood of his cross" (Col. 1:19).

And then, peace is the companion of knowing and doing the truth. We all know the agitated feeling that comes when we fail to speak the truth or act out the implication of a truth we hold. Matthew Henry said that peace was such a precious jewel he would give anything for it but the truth. Luther was taken captive of the Word of God. He could not act against what the Holy Spirit had revealed in Scripture. He had peace in the midst of immense turmoil because he followed the truth as he saw it.

Peace will be evicted from our hearts whenever we deny what we know is right or go along with a contradiction of what we believe. We cannot fly in the face of truth and still soar in joyous living. That presses me to ask myself and you: are we compromising in any area; are we contributing to society's denial of personhood to anyone; are we accepting mediocrity in the church which is sapping its power?

Further, peace is the result of a surrendered heart. Paul challenged the Colossians to "let the peace of Christ rule in [their] hearts" (Col. 3:15). The Greek word for *rule* means literally to act as an umpire: The indwelling Christ calls the shots. He rules on what's best and right for us and will keep us at peace. As the umpire of our hearts he sorts out our feelings and helps us to deal with anger, irritation, and annoyance. We can lift up all our attitudes for his judgment. When we are pressed by too many demands, he can help us decide what's important to bring us closer to him and fulfill his purpose for us.

There is a serene peace in us when we place ourselves under the Lord's authority and surrender all our affairs, decisions, and possibilities to him. Isaiah was right: "Thou dost keep him in perfect peace, whose mind is stayed on thee, because he trusts in thee" (Isa. 26:3). The only things that can deny us peace are those people and situations we do not completely surrender to the Lord. The peace of Christ is not the absence of turmoil or difficulty, but undeviating devotion to the will of God.

Added to that, peace is the result of a protected heart. Paul helped us to understand that in his classic statement to the Philippians: "Have no anxiety about anything, but in everything by prayer and supplication with thanksgiving let your requests be made known to God. And the peace of God, which passes all understanding, will keep your hearts and your minds in Christ Jesus" (Phil. 4:6–7). The word for *keep* means garrison, to look out for, to see before. The Lord is a sentinel for our hearts. When we know his peace, he helps us by protecting us against anything which would disrupt the harmonious and ordered functioning of our unified, knit-together hearts. He goes before us breaking trail, warning us of anything which would destroy our wholeness in him.

That is beyond understanding, certainly beyond our grand-est expectation or deserving!

Paul grappled with the mystery of how Christ had done that for him repeatedly. He was protected in danger, upheld in conflict and sealed against evil intrusion. When he ex-claimed about that peace which passes understanding, he was acknowledging that it is a mystery all our skill and knowledge cannot contrive or produce. Yet he knew that the peace of God had persistently protected and garrisoned his heart. I know that to be true. The peace of God has shielded me in im-possible pressures and anxieties. I have learned to claim the Lord's promise for Jerusalem in Zechariah's prophecy as the protection for my mind and heart. "For I will be to her a wall of fire round about, says the Lord, and I will be the glory within her" (Zech. 2:5). Then I can pray with Whittier: "Take from our souls the strain and stress/and let our ordered lives confess/the beauty of thy peace."[1]

But peace cannot be kept unless it is shared. We are not to keep the peace, but give it away. Peace is the result of peacemaking. The climax of the Beatitudes is "Blessed are the peacemakers, for they shall be called the sons of God."

A child shares the character and purpose of his father. We are truly sons and daughters of God when we are engaged in active peacemaking. That implies initiating reconciliation even when we think we're right and have been wronged. It

---

[1]John Greenleaf Whittier, "Dear Lord and Father of Mankind," 1872.

also means bringing estranged people together and helping them to find peace.

Anything which keeps people apart is the concern and responsibility of a peacemaker. If we want peace in our own hearts, negative criticism, gossip, and innuendos are no longer part of our conversation. Our constant concern is what will help people understand, forgive, and accept each other.

A friend underlined this for me the other day. He said, "I've searched for peace all during my Christian life. I tried to find peace in confession and in keeping a clear conscience. Then the Lord put on my conscience a greater sin than any of the little sins I kept fussing about. He told me that I was responsible to help bring peace into all the misunderstanding and angry hostility among people around me. I've learned that being a reconciler is essential for a continued, sustained experience of peace." The man was on target!

"God was in Christ reconciling the world to himself, not counting their trespasses against them, and entrusting to us the message of reconciliation. So we are ambassadors for Christ, God making his appeal through us" (2 Cor. 5:19–20).

Lastly, peace is the result of the indwelling of the Holy Spirit. Paul calls peace a fruit of the Spirit (Gal. 5:23). It is a manifestation of the living Christ, the Holy Spirit, working through us. Peace is the presence of the Lord in our hearts and minds. John's oft-repeated plea for us to abide in Christ and allow Christ to abide in us is the secret of prolonged, lasting peace. There is no finer gift which could close the letter from the Beloved Disciple and the Apostle of Love.

But wait! John has one last word. "The friends greet you. Greet the friends, every one of them." John wanted the church to pass on the peace. His concern to the end was that they should "love one another as Christ had loved them."

There's a lovely story about the elder John in the last year of his life. He was carried into the fellowship of the church, and his message was predictable. Though he was frail in body, his spirit was indomitable. With strong, unwavering voice he said, "Little children, love one another."

A bright, but impetuous young deacon asked, "Why do you always repeat the same message?" John's response was, "That's all you need to know!"

I am convinced he was right. Peace be with you!

PRAYER FOR THE DAY: *Gracious God, thank you for offering us the magnificent gift of peace. In the quiet, as we conclude this time in the letters of John, we want to confess the things that keep us from peace. Help us to accept your forgiveness, forgive ourselves, and express forgiveness to others. We commit our lives to love others as you have loved us. Abide in us, dear God, and love through us. Thank you for the peace that is beyond our understanding, which floods our hearts right now. In Christ's name and power. Amen.*

55 illus: distractions
55 note: for sermon on Lord's Prayer
161 quote: intercessory prayer
166 quote: idols

illus   18   sermon intro
illus   21   "Dishonesty"
39   illus: aging